THE MOST
MISUSED
STORIES
IN THE
BIBLE

THE MOST MISUSED STORIES IN THE BIBLE

SURPRISING WAYS POPULAR BIBLE STORIES ARE MISUNDERSTOOD

ERIC J. BARGERHUFF

BETHANYHOUSE
a division of Baker Publishing Group
Minneapolis, Minnesota

© 2017 by Eric J. Bargerhuff

Published by Bethany House Publishers
11400 Hampshire Avenue South
Bloomington, Minnesota 55438
www.bethanyhouse.com

Bethany House Publishers is a division of
Baker Publishing Group, Grand Rapids, Michigan

Printed in the United States of America

Library of Congress Cataloging-in-Publication Data is on file at the Library
of Congress in Washington, DC.

ISBN 978-0-7642-1913-9

Unless otherwise indicated, Scripture quotations are from the Holman Christian Standard Bible, copyright 1999, 2000, 2002, 2003 by Holman Bible Publishers. Used by permission.

Scripture quotations identified ESV are from The Holy Bible, English Standard
Version® (ESV®), copyright © 2001 by Crossway, a publishing ministry of
Good News Publishers. Used by permission. All rights reserved. ESV Text
Edition: 2007

Scripture quotations identified NASB are from the New American Standard
Bible®, copyright © 1960, 1962, 1963, 1968, 1971, 1972, 1973, 1975, 1977,
1995 by The Lockman Foundation. Used by permission.

Scripture identified NIV1984 is taken from the HOLY BIBLE, NEW INTER-
NATIONAL VERSION®. Copyright © 1973, 1978, 1984 Biblica. Used by
permission of Zondervan. All rights reserved.

Scripture quotation identified NKJV is from the New King James Version®.
Copyright © 1982 by Thomas Nelson, Inc. Used by permission. All rights reserved.

All italics in Scripture, added for emphasis, are the author's.

Cover design by Rob Williams, InsideOutCreativeArts

17 18 19 20 21 22 23   7 6 5 4 3 2 1

To those who hunger and thirst for truth,
may this book merely be an appetizer that leads you
to the main course—the inerrant, infallible,
timeless, and eternal Word of God.

I wish to also dedicate this book to the memory of Dr. Donald Rinehart, my religion professor at Ashland University in Ashland, Ohio. Don's passion for the Word, his love of college students, his perpetual smile, and his Barnabas-style spirit were a blessing to everyone who met him. Grace flowed through his life to so many. Thank you, Dr. Rinehart. The fact that you now see the Savior brings us great joy.

CONTENTS

Contents

INTRODUCTION

Everybody loves a good story, and the Bible has plenty of them. Some are shocking, some convicting. Still others are powerful in that they communicate truths about God and us like nothing else can.

But stories can often be misunderstood. They can be taken out of context. Details missed. Personal agendas read into them. Human traditions can cloud facts. Main points can be sidestepped or overlooked. Pertinent information from reliable and biblically accurate resources that could bring clarity can be ignored. Language can be misunderstood. Mistakes made.

This is why it is important for every Bible reader, from the serious student to the casual reader, to learn how to interpret the Bible in context, using all the aids and guides to faithful study. This—along with the accompanying power of the Holy Spirit and the Spirit-filled community of the church—will help us read and apply God's Word faithfully.

This book takes some of the most commonly misused stories of the Bible and puts them in context with the hope of bringing clarity and light to what God wants for our lives. It could be considered a companion to my previous book, *The Most Misused Verses in the Bible*. To be sure, there is commonality and overlap in the principles that I seek to teach, but the stories and texts of Scripture I deal with are different in each book.

I realize some may want to argue that this or that story should not have been included over others. All of this, of course, is a subjective decision pertaining to one's experience in life and in the church. By no means are these the most misused stories for *everyone*.

I do believe, however, that pointing out the common misuses and misunderstandings of these stories can lead to similar discoveries and application points to other Bible stories not covered in this book.

It is increasingly evident that we now live in a biblically ignorant culture that sees the Bible as outdated, old-fashioned, biased, political, and offensive to modern-day sensitivities and views. It may be surprising to hear that this is no different from the worldview of the Roman Empire, where paganism, immorality, and relativistic philosophy were commonplace. In many ways, the church is moving back toward the culture of the first century, where the persecuted church thrived.

For us, this means the light of the Bible and its message stand in contrast to the darkness prevalent in today's culture. We seem to be in Babylon once again. Biblical Christians will stand out against the prevailing tide of culture in ways that will naturally invite hostility and ridicule, perhaps even physical suffering at some point. But Christians who long to please and be faithful to God know that we have no choice but to follow the Bible's teachings as we seek to deliver the good news of the gospel of Jesus Christ to a lost world. At times it may be tempting to smooth the rough edges of biblical truth so that we are more readily received by the world. But to do so would be to compromise the timeless and eternal truths that set God's people apart from a perishing world. To do so would mean to forfeit the blessing of God that comes from obeying these truths in his Word. We must remain faithful to his truth no matter the times or the climate we find ourselves in. The Bible is not merely a historical record of God's redemption, but a living and active means of appropriating that redemption.

I invite you to read this book with a humble willingness to be challenged. Perhaps you will learn something new, or maybe I will simply be reinforcing what you already know and do naturally when it comes to reading the Scriptures. Maybe you will want to argue some point. Either way, may you read these stories anew with fresh eyes and may your heart be encouraged to hunger for and dive deeper into the Word of God.

If on some point you think differently than I do, I ask that we be mutually charitable while seeking more light on the subject. In the course of my life, I have misused a verse or story myself, and thankfully there was someone with a willing, graceful spirit to show me new insights that clarified God's Word for me. We are all students of the Bible, even those who have been trained and hold advanced degrees in Bible and theology. There must be what my dissertation mentor, Kevin Vanhoozer, calls a "hermeneutical humility" when reading ancient and sacred texts. In other words, if we are using a consistent, literal, historical, grammatical approach to interpretation and God brings new understanding to his Word, we all must be willing to learn and grow and even change our minds.

This means, knowing our own philosophical and cultural biases, we seek to interpret Scripture without those biases becoming a hindrance if they conflict with biblical truth. It means we learn to interpret the text in the context of a Spirit-filled community, the body of Christ. It means we allow God's Word to master us more than we seek to master it.

We stand on the shoulders of church tradition and thousands of years of interpretation. It would be chronological snobbery to think we are the only ones who have the best insights into the truth. Some of the greatest and most insightful discoveries have come from theologians, pastors, and laypeople who have lived out, taught, preached, and written about these truths throughout the centuries. We would do well to become acquainted with them in our task of interpreting and applying the unchanging truth of the gospel to our lives today.

Like my previous book, this book can serve as a daily devotional guide, a book for small-group study, or as a side text for courses on how to interpret the Bible. I've seen some pastors use the idea for a sermon series, and I have seen people simply read it for a quick, casual read. Either way, my prayer is that it will be profitable for you on your spiritual journey.

The Bible is a life-changing book, but if misinterpreted and misused, it can become a dangerous book. How we view God has a direct impact on how we live, what we think and believe, how we feel, and how we treat others. So it is all the more important that we seek to understand who God is and what his will for us is in keeping with the truth he has revealed in his Word.

Now let's look at some of the most misused stories in the Bible, reading stories that are all full of grace and truth, stories that ultimately point to Christ and his redeeming love for you and me.

1

David and Goliath

"You come to me with a sword, a spear, and a javelin, but I come to you in the name of the Lord of hosts."

—1 Samuel 17:45 NASB

Growing up, my friends and I loved to play Little League baseball. One advantage of living in a small town was that I could ride my bicycle to and from the ball field for practices and games. I would slide my mitt over the handlebars and pedal my way through town, proudly wearing my multicolored Astros uniform.

When I played, I was never afraid of the baseball and getting hurt. But before or after games, it was a different story. My bike ride always took me by a house that had a rather large Doberman pinscher with a huge bark and equally large teeth. I'm not sure if it was me, the color of my uniform, the bike I was riding, or the feeding schedule he was on, but whenever he saw me, he ran to the full length of his chain and practically choked himself, ready to tear me to pieces. You can imagine how fast my heart beat and pedals moved whenever I neared his yard.

Now, generally speaking, dogs don't scare me—but this guy was the exception. He was looking for a steak, and I fit the profile. But as long as he was on that chain, I was fine. I actually came to enjoy the adrenaline rush as I rode past his yard, and occasionally would even give a few fake barks of my own in his general direction. (We all have our ways of dealing with fear.)

But on one occasion, the man-eater's owner happened to be untying him from the chain at the very moment I came by. It was then that my worst nightmare became a reality. With unbridled speed and red rage surging through his eyes, that Doberman broke free from his master's grip and charged at me with fury in his bark and saliva flying from his mouth.

The words *panic*, *terror*, *horror*, and *"I'm too young to die"* don't begin to describe the fear that instantly gripped my soul as my eyes grew big and my stomach grew nauseated watching this beast approach. In a flash, the dog was biting at my pedals and barking at full volume. I let out such a blood-curdling yell that I'm sure the entire population of Mexico, Indiana, heard it.

With my feet dangling and kicking, my handlebars out of control, and my hat flying off my head, the dog's owner yelled not at the dog but at me to stop the bike and be still! What was he thinking? I wasn't about to stop and become this animal's dessert. But I had no choice because my feet slipped off the pedals and my bike came crashing to the ground. I hit the ground hard and covered my head with my hands. But to my surprise, the black beast pulled up from his jet-fighter attack and sprinted back to his owner with a stride of fulfillment that undoubtedly made him a hero in his own mind.

The owner asked if I was okay, but I couldn't say a word. I quickly grabbed my hat, picked up my bike, and raced down the street while trying to catch my breath and restart my heart. It was the closest I had ever come to dying in the short twelve years I had been alive.

It is, as they say, a memory and a feeling I will never forget.

Fear is a powerful reminder of our mortality, and it is the very thing that can render us paralyzed and numb when faced with important decisions or interactions with intimidating people (and Doberman pinschers).

Many will tell us that when we are afraid, we should simply pull ourselves up by our bootstraps and face "the giant" before us with the confidence we muster up from deep within—whether the giant is a roller coaster, a final exam at school, or a relationship gone sour. And if there was ever a biblical story that would seem to fit that mandate, it is the story of David and Goliath.

The story of the shepherd boy versus the giant Philistine warrior in 1 Samuel 17 is known worldwide. From Sunday school to sermons, we are taught to face our fears like David did and stare down the giants that wage war against our souls. But is this the best way to understand and apply the story of David and Goliath?

I say the story is not about David overcoming fear. If you look closer, you see that he shows no signs of fear at all. In fact, David is quite confident (and quite perturbed) when he hears about this unusually large warrior who seemingly has lassoed the armies of Israel with his thundering voice and intimidating presence.

The Israelites, led by their first king, Saul, were encamped in a valley. They had drawn up battle lines against their arch-enemies, the Philistines, who were led by a "champion named Goliath of Gath" (17:4 ESV). Estimated at nine feet nine inches tall, he had armor, a javelin, and a spear, the head of which weighed some fifteen pounds.

Goliath issued a bold challenge to Saul and his army, saying he would fight anyone who would come meet him in battle, and if he lost, the Philistines would become their servants. But if Goliath prevailed, Saul and his men would lay down their arms and become servants to the Philistines.

Goliath was defying the ranks of Israel with his nasty, intimidating bark. But then a young boy comes by, a shepherd named David on a mission from his father. David was a part-time armor-bearer for Saul, so he was used to coming on and off the battlefield and returning home regularly to care for his father's sheep.

But on this latest trip to the battlefield, David was given an assignment by his father to carry some grain and bread to three of his older brothers who were enlisted full-time in Saul's army. In addition, David was to take ten cheeses to their commander (incidentally, one of only a few times cheese is mentioned in the Bible).

Now as David approached the armies of Israel and greeted his brothers, who had once again aligned against the Philistines, he heard the familiar voice and taunt of the monster-warrior Goliath repeating the same challenge he had been giving for forty days and forty nights.

David watched as the men of Israel fled in fear, even though King Saul had apparently offered a reward—great riches and his daughter in marriage—to any man who would stand up to the giant and bring him down. David was grieved when he saw this, and poignantly asked, "Who is this uncircumcised Philistine, that he should defy the armies of the living God?" (1 Samuel 17:26 ESV).

David did not seem to register any fear, and his bold words eventually reached the attention of King Saul, who called for him to come and report to him. Then David said to the king, "Don't let anyone be discouraged by him; your servant will go and fight this Philistine!" (17:32).

Saul doubted David's capabilities, but David convinced him he was able due to his past victories in striking down lions and bears in defense of his father's sheep. Now David was asserting himself once again to defend another group of scared sheep, the armies of Israel. To David, Goliath was just another lion or bear to be conquered, and he was confident God would deliver him from the hand of this Philistine brute as well.

The king gave his consent, and then tried to give David his armor for further protection. But David was not about to wear it. He was to find victory in being himself and trusting in the God he knew was sovereign over man and all living things. So with staff and stones and sling in hand, he made his way out to the Philistine to make it clear whose God was in charge.

The mockery came quickly, with Goliath taunting David, "Am I a dog that you come against me with sticks?" (17:43). He then cursed David, no doubt hoping he would shrink back in fear. But once again, David showed no fear:

"You come to me with a sword, a spear, and a javelin, but I come to you in the name of the Lord of hosts, the God of the armies of Israel, whom you have taunted. This day the Lord will deliver you up into my hands, and I will strike you down and remove your head from you. And I will give the dead bodies of the army of the Philistines this day to the birds of the sky and the wild beasts of the earth, that all the earth may know that there is a God in Israel, and that all this assembly may know that the Lord does not deliver by sword or by spear; for the battle is the Lord's and He will give you into our hands."

17:45–47 NASB

These are hardly the words of a boy who is afraid of a big dog.

And most of us know the rest of the story. David quickly approached Goliath (again, with no fear), pulled a stone from his bag, and slung it with such precision that it struck the middle of Goliath's forehead, sending him to the ground. With that, David retrieved the giant's sword and finished him off.

You see, David had a history with God. And because David knew the character and power of his God, he had no fear. To be fair, fear *is* a part of this story. The irony is that the ones who truly were afraid (Saul and his army) chose not to battle the giant. They certainly did not overcome fear with faith.

But David, the one without fear, overcame the giant not because he wanted to conquer his fear, but because he was zealous to defend the character and glory of God. So the main point of the story is not about overcoming fear and facing your giants as much as it is about trusting in the power and character of God to deliver.

When God's reputation is on the line, and a man or woman of faith seeks to defend his honor, you can rest assured that God will be there. God will be glorified in the life of one who trusts in him. He will deliver his people and ultimately triumph, for he gives us the victory, either in this life or in the life to come.

2

Gideon and His Fleece

"I will be with you," the Lord said to him. "You
will strike Midian down as if it were one man."

—Judges 6:16

College can be such a great time in life. Freedom,
friends, and, yes, hard, disciplined study is the stuff
that memories are made of. I graduated from a small
liberal arts college in Ohio, and can remember well those
initial classes each semester when professors would take at-
tendance, asking each student to give their name, where they
were from, and their major area of study. In those early years
I was a little frustrated because I knew my name, where I
was from, but . . . my major?

At one point I thought getting a criminal justice degree and
returning to my home state of Indiana to be a state trooper

was a good option. Journalism was another possibility, since I enjoyed writing and had served as editor-in-chief of my high school newspaper. Fortunately, with so many required general education classes the first few years of school, I didn't feel too much pressure to declare a major. Eventually, however, I would have to make a decision.

As a growing Christian, I wanted to know *God's will* on the matter. I believed he had a plan for me, I just didn't know what it was. Friends and loved ones didn't hesitate to give me advice. Some talked about throwing out a "fleece" to discern the will of God.

They were speaking figuratively, of course. They weren't telling me to toss out a wool blanket or shear a sheep. The idea of using a fleece to test God's will comes from the Old Testament story of Gideon, in Judges 6.

The story goes like this: The Israelites—less than one generation after God had delivered them from slavery in Egypt and led them to the promised land—were already rebelling against God. They had fallen victim to the allure of pagan religions and practices that surrounded them and became morally and spiritually compromised, all because they had disobeyed God's command to conquer and drive the Canaanites out of the land. Scripture says the generation that followed Joshua "did not know the Lord or the works He had done for Israel" (Judges 2:10). They turned their backs on God, began worshiping idols, and failed to follow the commands of Moses as set forth in the Law of God.

Deeply grieved and angered, God lifted his hand of protection and blessing from the Israelites and allowed the surrounding peoples to pillage and enslave them, even to the point where it is said "the Lord was against them."[1] Their

Deliverer and Redeemer had now become their enemy because of their faithless rebellion, and they suffered greatly.

But Israel, in desperation, cried out to the one true God to rescue them again, and because he is full of grace, he had pity on them. The Lord rose up leader after leader, known as *judges*, to help deliver the Israelites from their enemies. God's people would follow the Lord for a while, but due to their lack of true repentance, soon after the judge died, they would once again slip back into their old corruption, becoming worse than they were before.

This pattern of deliverance followed by a descent into corruption and subsequent oppression by their enemies lasted hundreds of years. The common refrain throughout the book of Judges is "In those days there was no king in Israel; everyone did whatever he wanted" (Judges 17:6).

One of the judges raised up by God was a man named Gideon. The Midianites had been ravaging and oppressing Israel for seven years. Scripture tells us the angel of the Lord visited Gideon while he was threshing wheat in a wine vat (a low place in the ground for crushing grapes). The wine vat kept Gideon somewhat out of the sight of the Midianites, who might see him and be tempted to steal the grain.

It was here that the Angel of the LORD greeted Gideon: "The Lord is with you, mighty warrior" (6:12). Now, this was no ordinary greeting, and this was no ordinary angel. Later in the story the angel is identified as none other than God himself in temporary angelic form (vv. 14, 16, 23, 25, 27).[2] The Lord had chosen Gideon for a special task, and his time had come, but there were things in Gideon's heart that needed to be dealt with first.

Gideon feared the Midianites, which is why he was down in the vat in the first place. But he was also discouraged because what he knew to be true about God did not seem to match up with what he was experiencing. When the angel said, "The Lord is with you," Gideon responded, "Please Sir, if the Lord is with us, why has all this happened?" (v. 13).[3]

Gideon made the common mistake we make today—looking at our painful circumstances and using them to measure or draw false conclusions about the goodness and character of God. In a fallen world, where sin, death, and evil still exist, we should not expect the ideal paradise to be realized in this life, but rather in the life to come.

But Gideon didn't see it that way. He felt the Lord had abandoned his people, and he truly doubted what the angel was saying. The past seven years had been miserable. But Israel was being oppressed by the Midianites because of their own sin. We have the same tendency to look elsewhere or blame someone else for the mess we find ourselves in, just like Adam and Eve did in the garden of Eden.

Yet the angel, full of grace, had confidence in Gideon in spite of his doubt. The angel then *made God's will abundantly clear*, when he said, "Go in the strength you have and deliver Israel from the power of Midian. Am I not sending you?" (6:14). Still, Gideon wrestled with unbelief.

He said to Him, "Please, Lord, how can I deliver Israel? Look, my family is the weakest in Manasseh, and I am the youngest in my father's house."

"But I will be with you," the Lord said to him. "You will strike down Midian as if it were one man."

vv. 15–16

Each time Gideon had an objection, the angel countered with a confident assertion of God's will. And his patience was not going to run thin even in light of Gideon's next move: introducing his own set of tests in order to see some physical proof of whether the angel was genuinely telling the truth.

Gideon asked for a sign, and offered a gift of bread, meat, and broth to the angel who consumed it with fire before disappearing instantly. Panicked and fearing he had truly seen God and would surely die, Gideon cried out and once again received the reassuring word from God that he should not fear and would not die.[4] Again, God was being patient.

Eventually, Gideon began to move in the direction of obedience, but he still had his doubts, and therefore had one more "test" for God, this one involving fleeces.

> Then Gideon said to God, "If You will deliver Israel by my hand, as You said, I will put a fleece of wool here on the threshing floor. If dew is only on the fleece, and all the ground is dry, I will know that You will deliver Israel by my strength, as You said."
>
> vv. 36–37

Notice that Gideon is stating what God's will already is because he had previously heard God tell him—noted by the words "You said" in the verses above. And sure enough, God patiently endured Gideon's doubt by going along with the test, wetting the fleece overnight while keeping the ground dry. You would think it would be enough.

But here we go again. Gideon's weak faith (which is still better than no faith) put God to the test again, and he asked

God to do the opposite the next day—keep the fleece dry and make the ground wet. And sure enough, the next day it was as he asked.

Finally, Gideon had enough physical proof to be convinced, and he moved forward with an army in an attempt to ambush the Midianites. As the story goes, God cut back Gideon's army to just three hundred men, nearly impossible odds, since they would clearly be outnumbered. But God did this so that God alone would get the glory for the victory.

Gideon's army surrounded the Midianites at night. The ambush plan involved torches and trumpets and shattered pitchers, such that the Midianites were so taken aback, confused, and frightened that they killed each other while many others ran crying out in fear.

At the end of the day, Gideon was victorious, but it seemed like a long process to get there. And the question then comes: Are Gideon's fleece tests meant to be a pattern for us today to discern the will of God? Should we be looking for signs and physical proof by putting God to the test in order to make sure we know God's heart on a matter?

I assert that this is not a healthy pattern for us to imitate. First, Gideon *already knew the will of God* because it came to him via God's Word. The angel told him directly what God's plans were. Though we don't have angels speaking to us today, we certainly have a full and complete record of God's Word in our Bibles, and we would do well to seek God and to hear his voice in the pages of Scripture so that we can take heed to what God has already stated is his will for us.

Only then will we begin to develop the "mind of God" in such a way that we can think and act more like him. The Bible says, "Be joyful always, pray continually, give thanks in all circumstances; for this is God's will for you in Christ Jesus" (1 Thessalonians 5:16–18 NIV1984).

With this in mind, it is clear that God in many places has already revealed much of his will. But if we are not seeking to obey God in those areas, what makes us think God would be eager to show us his will in things that pertain to decisions that fall outside the pages of Scripture?

I'm not suggesting we have to be morally perfect in order to discern the will of God in other areas of our life. That won't be possible while we live in this flesh in this fallen world. But I am suggesting that God wants us to "seek first the kingdom of God and his righteousness" (Matthew 6:33), and all these other cares of life will be added to us in his own perfect timing.

We must be more consumed with pursuing the *person* of God than pursuing the *will* of God. In a subtle way, even our pursuit of God's will could become an idol if it eclipses our pursuit of simply knowing and obeying God as an act of worship. God delights when we are in his will, and he wants us to be in it even more than we do.

In his delightful book about discerning the will of God, *Found: God's Will*, pastor and teacher John MacArthur argues that if we are saved, seeking to be Spirit-filled, sanctified (set apart for God), submissive to authority, and willing to suffer for Christ in a hostile world, then God will be shaping and forming the desires of our hearts that we should pursue.

MacArthur does an excellent job of calling us to "get into the mainstream of what God is doing and let Him lead you to that perfect will."[5] This means knowing, worshiping, and serving God should be the primary goals of our lives while also denying the fleshly tendencies that often wage war against us. In so doing, we will often find ourselves and our desires in alignment with what God's will is for us. We can then make the choice and pursue it.

I firmly believe that to discern the will of God, we should study the Word and pray while seeking out godly counsel from mature people who know God and his biblical principles—people who know us well. When we develop a discerning heart and live in the power of the Spirit, forsaking sin, and truly seeking to please God, he will make his will clear to us. He will shape our desires, and when we make a choice, we can be confident he will lead us in the right path.

Guessing games that use signs and fleeces are meant to put God to the test, and only prove we are insecure like Gideon was. Instead, seeking first his kingdom and his righteousness will fortify your soul with confidence in a God who wants you to delight in him first. It is then that all the other things "will be provided for you" (Matthew 6:33).

So get rid of the fleece. Ditch the pursuit of signs in the sky or reading into situations what ought not to be read into for the purpose of finding God's will. Desiring these kinds of discernment tactics should be a red flag, reminding us we are not walking with God closely enough to have him shape the desires of our hearts. As my favorite Old Testament "discernment" verses say, "Trust in the Lord with all your heart, and do not lean on your own understanding. In all your ways acknowledge him, and he will make straight your paths" (Proverbs 3:5–6 ESV).

"Delight yourself in the Lord, and he will give you the desires of your heart. Commit your way to the Lord; trust in him, and he will act" (Psalm 37:4–5 ESV).

29

3

Cain and Abel

And the Lord said, "What have you done? The voice of your brother's blood is crying to me from the ground."

—Genesis 4:10 ESV

Most of us have an acute sense of justice. If anything has even a hint of being unfair, it drives us crazy. To be sure, we are designed this way, but there is truly a realm where the battle for fairness can quickly rise to a fever pitch of emotional intensity: sibling rivalry.

Whether between brothers, between sisters, or between sisters and brothers, it doesn't matter; the intensity of the rivalry can far exceed anything man can make up—from Pepsi vs. Coke, Red Sox vs. Yankees, or an Indiana vs. Purdue basketball game. Just ask any parent who hears the nearly constant comparing of the size of ice-cream servings, the number of trophies, or the grades on report cards.

Enter Cain and Abel, the world's first siblings, and a story that causes lots of confusion and debate in Christian circles. Their story is not so much misused as it is misunderstood. The crux of the storyline doesn't seem right or fair. Why is one brother's offering to God accepted while the other's is rejected? The surface reading raises many questions, requiring us to study harder and dig deeper.

As with other stories in the Bible, uncovering the context is critical. Dad and Mom (Adam and Eve) have made a huge mistake and plunged the universe and the human race into a fallen state through their disobedience in the garden of Eden. Evicted from the garden, where life was fruitful without effort, the first couple is now cast out of Paradise to work the ground and develop their own garden for survival's sake.[1]

Before this sin came into the world, Adam and Eve were commanded to be fruitful and multiply (Genesis 1:28), but this does not come to pass until after they are banished from the garden—so their children are born with the sin nature (and all who follow will as well). Two brothers are born from Adam and Eve's union. The first was named Cain, and the second Abel. We are not told the age difference; it is even possible they were twins. All we know from the text is this:

> Adam was intimate with his wife Eve, and she conceived and gave birth to Cain. She said, "I have had a male child with the Lord's help." Then she also gave birth to his brother Abel.
>
> Genesis 4:1–2

So far so good. But since the sin nature is passed on, it will soon show itself in the lives of these two boys whose early lives we are told nothing about. Though they come from the same stock, the boys are very different—one a farmer, the other a herder. Neither task should be seen as superior to the other, though many who read this story mistakenly come to that conclusion. Still, the differing occupations are the perfect seeds for some sort of rivalry, or in this case, an opportunity for jealousy to raise its ugly head.

An untold amount of time passes until we arrive at a good day gone bad.

> In the course of time Cain presented some of the land's produce as an offering to the Lord. And Abel also presented an offering—some of the firstborn of his flock and their fat portions. The Lord had regard for Abel and his offering, but He did not have regard for Cain and his offering.
>
> vv. 3–5

So the boys have given themselves to their select line of work and they bring the fruit of their labors before the Lord as an offering to him. God likes the one, but rejects the other, and this is the place where our feathers get ruffled. What gives? Cain brings a basket of organic fruit, vegetables, or grain as an offering, and Abel brings some high-quality meats. Again, both offerings would be honorable, so a closer read is needed to shed light on the subject.

Notice that Moses (the writer of Genesis) points out that Cain brought "some of the land's produce," whereas Abel brought "some of the firstborn of his flock and their fat portions." It would seem that Abel's offering was the best of an animal that could never produce that offering portion again (unlike the harvest from the ground), and therefore it may be perceived as a greater and costlier offering.[2]

Could this have made Cain's offering somehow inferior in God's sight? Scripture doesn't record for us if God gave special instructions for the sacrifice, but could it also be that Abel presented his offering properly and Cain didn't? It's possible, but that seems to be conjecture—an argument from silence. We simply are not given those details.

Are there other clues? Yes. I suggest this likely comes down to a *heart issue*. Many scholars take a big-picture look at Genesis and conclude that Cain was "self-absorbed"[3] and had an attitude problem, and that this may have been what God was responding to when the two men brought their offerings to him. One brother was worshiping from the heart, and one was not, something that only God himself can see, which is why it makes it difficult for us, the reader, to understand since we don't know what God knows.

This conclusion is further supported when we read commentary on this event that comes later in the New Testament in the book of Hebrews. Notice how the writer describes Abel in the famous "wall of faith"—a summary of believers in biblical history who lived and worshiped by faith.

> By faith Abel offered to God a better sacrifice than Cain did. By faith he was approved as a righteous man, because God approved his gifts, and even though he is dead, he still speaks through his faith.
>
> Hebrews 11:4

It is obvious here that the words *faith* and *better sacrifice* inform one another. In other words, they modify each other. Because it was done in faith, Abel made a better sacrifice in God's sight. By implication then, Cain's sacrifice was not done in faith or with an attitude of worship. Therefore, God rejected it.

So the nature of the offering (whether grown in the ground or harvested from flocks) doesn't seem to be the problem. The problem comes from what was in each man's heart when the offering was given. Cain was going through the motions; Abel was worshiping in faith.

This lesson hits deep into the lives of those who claim to be followers of Christ today. Some go through the motions, others are genuine. Today, there are many in our churches who think they are genuine believers, but unfortunately they are not. They may have been raised in the church all their lives and therefore assume they are Christians. They may have all the right words, know a lot about the Bible and can quote much of it, have given themselves in service to others, and may even have a history of giving generously to the church. But unless their hearts have been changed, "born again" by the Holy Spirit through genuine repentance and saving faith in Jesus, they can be tragically self-deceived.

This is a painful subject to bring up, but it is one reason why the church today is often as weak as it is and why many so-called "Christians" don't truly act like Christians. *The gospel of God's grace needs to be explicitly preached and taught so that desperate hearts stand a chance of experiencing real life transformation and change.* We have to proclaim the truth about the life, death, and resurrection of Jesus Christ and the need for sinners like you and me to repent and believe that God in Christ has provided atonement for and forgiveness of our sins through the cross.

But when this is not the central message of the church, it becomes weak, people are sold a lie, and "going through the motions" and "playing church" become the norm. It becomes nothing more than a religious social club with some humanitarian causes mixed in.

But the Bible is clear; we are only Christians when we genuinely believe we are *saved by grace through faith*—a faith that is real, with its object being Jesus Christ—a faith that cannot be faked or manufactured. Behavior modification does not save us, speaking Christianese (using Christian terms and phrases) does not save us, giving money and serving humankind does not save us, and getting baptized (a human action) does not save us. Outward actions are all insufficient. Only faith, in the heart, given as a gift by the Holy Spirit (Ephesians 2:8–9) can save us, and then human actions prompted and empowered by the Spirit proceed from that.

Only the kind of faith that turns from sin and turns toward Christ has the power to transform a heart, to bring it from death to life, from darkness to light. Otherwise, we are lost and still living by our fleshly sinful nature. And no matter how religious-looking or -sounding someone might be, if they are merely going through the motions, God will know it.

Cain and Abel's story is a perfect example of God seeing the heart behind the "religious activity." Humans look at outward things, but God looks on the heart (1 Samuel 16:7). He knows who loves him and those who love themselves. He knows who is coming to him out of duty instead of faith.

Cain's *lack* of faith—the transforming kind I am talking about—was not only evident in his offering, but his lack of faith and disdain for God and his commands resurfaced later in what we now know to be the first murder recorded in Scripture. Though God had warned Cain about the dangers of sin, Cain let the sin in his heart overtake him, and out of jealousy and pride he took his brother's life.

And when God called out to him and asked him where Abel was, he uttered the now famous sarcastic response, "Am I my brother's keeper?" (Genesis 4:9 ESV). Thus Cain, the man who merely went through the motions in his relationship with God, revealed his true nature and character after he was "called out" about his empty offering.

Instead of responding to God in repentance and faith, Cain reacted violently to his embarrassment and shame, killed his brother, lied about his whereabouts, and responded sarcastically to God when called on to give an account.

So we too can soften our hearts, fall at the Lord's feet in repentance, and receive his mercy and grace, or we can harden our hearts, live a self-deceived life, and ratify the sin nature we're born with. We can become resistant to God's authority and brush off God and his commands with an attitude that is bent toward self—just like Cain did.

The contrast couldn't be clearer. One man worships in faith while the other merely pretends to do so. But *who you are* is far more important than *what you do*. One is a matter of the heart; the other is an activity that will have no eternal value unless it is done in faith.

What I like about Cain and Abel's story is that it also provides us with an excellent example of how to interpret the Bible correctly. Though there are some clues in the Genesis 4 account as to why God may have rejected Cain's offering and accepted Abel's, we can learn much more when we use a cross-reference, like the one in Hebrews 11, to shed more light on the event so that we can draw some healthy conclusions.

Scripture actually helps us interpret Scripture, because behind the scenes all of it is inspired by the same author, the Holy Spirit. He used different writers, but he inspired the very words in the Bible—words from God's heart. It was not given through divine dictation, but rather God used the very personalities, experiences, and expressions of each writer to shape the inspired text into what God intended.

Therefore, Hebrews 11 sheds brilliant light on the events of Genesis 4. We are not told that Abel presented a better offering, but that he presented a better *sacrifice*. The sacrifice of Abel's offering done in faith ultimately foreshadowed the cross of Christ, the sacrifice that atoned for our sin. Therefore, as the author of Hebrews rightly says, Abel's life and sacrifice "still speaks" to us today, in the sense that the biblical story teaches us how to approach God in faith for what he has done through the sacrifice of Christ.

Though the story did not end well for Abel (at least on the earthly side), it didn't end well for Cain either. He was once again confronted by God about his sin, and God subsequently set forth serious consequences. He was cursed. He no longer had the privilege of farming the soil, the life that brought him joy. *His sin robbed him of his joy.*

Instead, he wandered the face of the earth, driven from the life that fulfilled into an emptiness that never satisfied. Similarly, people today will never find true satisfaction in the life they were designed to have until they find it first in a relationship with their Maker and Redeemer.

Professor of Old Testament and theology Victor Hamilton writes about Cain's banishment,

In some ways it is a fate worse than death. It is to lose all sense of belonging and identification with a community. It is to become rootless and detached. Perhaps we, the readers, should at this point view Cain not so much as a villain but as a tragic character. Cain, once a farmer, is now ousted from civilization and is to become a vagabond. Rootlessness is the punishment and the wilderness is the refuge of the sinner.[4]

Indeed, it is a tragic story. Cain is discouraged, he feels the separation from God that sin brings, and ironically he fears for his life. But God spares him instant death, and puts a permanent mark on him so that no one who finds him will kill him. God is merciful to Cain, even though the mark would be a constant reminder of what he had done.

As the narrative concludes, we are told that "Cain went out from the presence of the Lord, and settled in the land of Nod, east of Eden" (Genesis 4:16 NASB). Kenneth Mathews, a biblical scholar on Genesis, notes that Nod is a play on the Hebrew word *nād,* which means "wanderer."[5] That makes Cain a wanderer wandering in the "land of the wanderer." Though one can never truly leave the Lord's presence (since he is omnipresent), the text clearly implies that Cain is separated and alienated in his relationship with God. He experiences, in some ways, a hell on earth. Later in Scripture, the apostle John will tell us that Cain "was of the evil one," a man whose "works were evil" while his "brother's were righteous" (1 John 3:12). Nothing could be sadder than belonging to the Evil One, or Satan.

But this is the reality for those who are not worshiping the one true God from the heart. We must get past the idea that people are safe simply because they look and act religious or do religious duties or are seemingly upright, moral people. We all need the gospel to bring us deliverance from sin and faith that leads to eternal life. Anything else is merely going through the motions, and to live that way is to live away from the presence of the Lord.

So let us walk by faith so that we may live a life that pleases God and offer ourselves in thanksgiving to the Lord. That is the kind of life that still speaks today.

4

Jonah and the Big Fish

"Salvation belongs to the Lord!"

—Jonah 2:9 ESV

I
f there is one story in the Bible that has captured the
imagination of children everywhere, it has to be the story
of Jonah.

Countless picture books, puzzles, and children's Bibles
have illustrated how Jonah the prophet ran away from God
and got swallowed by a big fish. Then, from the belly of the
fish (a whale?), he repented of his sin, was spit up on dry
land, and lived to have a successful preaching ministry.[1]

Even for adults, there's a lot to like about Jonah's story:
adventure, boats, storms, a huge fish, a rebellious runaway
prophet, guts and grime, a miraculous rescue, and a dramatic ending. But more than that, when you look closer at

the narrative, it's powerful, and I would argue it has God's redeeming love written all over it.

But Jonah's story is often misunderstood because the main emphasis is often put in the wrong place. The main theme is not about a fish, it's not about the city of Nineveh, and believe it or not, it's not even about Jonah. The story of Jonah is about God and his patient, loving grace and mercy; his relentless pursuit of sinners like you and me.

The book of Jonah is one of the twelve books in the Old Testament that we call the Minor Prophets; books including Hosea, Amos, Joel, Micah, and Malachi. Though they are called "minor prophets," there is nothing minor about them. Their prophecies are only minor *in length* as compared to the longer Major Prophets, like Isaiah, Jeremiah, or Ezekiel.

As for Jonah, it might surprise you to know that this is not the only place in the Bible where we learn about him. He is first mentioned as a prophet of God in the book of 2 Kings, where he successfully prophesied to the king of Israel that they should fortify the kingdom's boundaries to ward off an attack from their enemies.

And the Bible says that the Lord saved Israel from attack because the king listened to Jonah's prophecy. So Jonah was a legitimate prophet of God. Even the Jewish historian Josephus traces Jonah's life and ministry in Jewish history. But even if those things weren't enough, Jonah's credibility as a real historical prophet is confirmed by none other than Jesus Christ. In talking about his future death and resurrection, Jesus said, "For just as Jonah was three days and three nights in the belly of the great fish, so will the Son of Man be three days and three nights in the heart of the earth" (Matthew 12:40 ESV).

Therefore, even Jesus confirmed the historical nature of this story, and we cannot merely dismiss it as a fable. For here in Matthew, Jesus linked the promise of his own historical death and resurrection to the historicity of the story of Jonah. This factual Old Testament story served as an event that foreshadowed the purpose of Christ's mission to die and rise again.

But even if you have a hard time believing a fish swallowed a man and that he lived there for three days and three nights, let me remind you that the Bible is a supernatural book about a supernatural God who does supernatural things. Remember that Jesus was raised from the dead, and in Genesis 1, God created the world out of nothing. Making an air pocket for a man to survive inside a large fish doesn't seem hard compared to those things.

Jonah was given a mission, a calling. He was called by God in the eighth century BC to preach a message of repentance to a group of Assyrians in the city of Nineveh, the *archenemy* of the Israelites. But this didn't sit well with Jonah.

He hated the Assyrians. They were wicked pagans, who constantly waged war against God's chosen people, the Israelites. In Jonah's mind, the Assyrians were filthy, immoral, hedonistic people, who had no regard for the one true God. So why would God present an opportunity for mercy to the people who deserved judgment? And if God was merciful to the Assyrians, did this mean he had given up on and turned his back on the Israelites? Either way, Jonah didn't want anything to do with God's assignment for him.

So Jonah went in the opposite direction. The text says Jonah went down to the seaport of Joppa and sought to board a ship to the ancient city of Tarshish in order to escape "the presence of the Lord" (1:3 ESV). But as a prophet of God, he should have known better. No man can escape God's presence. But again, Jonah wasn't thinking straight. He was only thinking about himself.

In fact, one might even suggest that Jonah was mad at God, and therefore he chose to be outright rebellious and disobedient, which is what our human flesh tends to do when we are disillusioned with God. He knew the right thing to do, but didn't do it, which is sin (James 4:17).[2] Therefore, he got on a boat headed for a strange land, and it should have felt strange to him.

He should have said to himself, "I don't belong here . . ." And in the same way today, if we are is looking at a nasty computer site or watching a filthy movie or sitting with that group of people who are gossiping about someone else, we should say to ourselves, "I don't belong here," and then do something about it.

However, Jonah boarded the ship anyway and set sail. But God pursued him because that's what the Bible is about: God's radical, pursuing grace in the midst of rebellion. God hurled a great big storm at the ship, such a powerful storm that the seasoned sailors were afraid and started crying out to their own gods for help. None of this seemed to concern Jonah, though, because he was down in the ship sleeping. And he didn't care!

One can't help but see the downward direction of Jonah at this point. The text says Jonah *went down* to Joppa (1:3), and then Jonah *went down* to the inner part of the ship, and from there Jonah *lay down* and was fast asleep. It seems like all along Jonah keeps going on this downward spiral, and if something doesn't change pretty soon, the ship's going down too. Sin doesn't lift you up, it only brings you down, and Jonah is circling the drain.

But the captain woke him up and essentially said, "Get up, slacker! We're going to be goners! Cry out to your God. We're crying out to ours. Maybe one of these gods will hear us and spare us!" But Jonah knew why this was happening. He was to blame. And when the sailors figured it out too, they demanded an answer from him.

Here again is where Jonah himself testified to the one all-powerful and true living God.

> And he said to them, "I am a Hebrew, and I fear the Lord, the God of heaven, who made the sea and the dry land." Then the men were exceedingly afraid and said to him, "What is this that you have done!" For the men knew that he was fleeing from the presence of the Lord, because he had told them.
>
> Jonah 1:9–10 ESV

Jonah admits he is running away from "the God of heaven, who made the *sea* and the *dry land*." He is running away from the one true God, who is sovereign over storms because he is the Maker of the land and the sea. He is running away from the God, who is continuing to pursue Jonah even in his rebellion. This terrifies the sailors all the more because they realize that all of this is happening because of Jonah.

But instead of repenting of his rebellion and sin on the spot, Jonah surprisingly decides he would just as soon die, and he suggests to the sailors that throwing him overboard into the sea will make it quiet down because this is all his fault. Unfortunately, his pride and shame have kept him from coming back to God, a familiar theme for many people who once claimed to walk with God but seemingly have walked away.

Jonah is disgusted with God. He's disgusted with the Ninevites, and he's disgusted with himself. So he'd rather die. But the sailors don't think that killing a follower of the Sovereign God of the sea is such a good idea, so they struggle desperately to row back to land, to no avail.

Rather quickly, they've come to fear the Lord themselves, and they decide to do what Jonah has said to do: toss him overboard. But before they do, they ask God not to punish them. They see their gods as useless, but Jonah's God is a God of action. Remarkably, they have a healthier reverence for God than Jonah does.

> So they picked up Jonah and hurled him into the sea, and the sea ceased from its raging. Then the men feared the Lord exceedingly, and they offered a sacrifice to the Lord and made vows.
>
> Jonah 1:15–16 ESV

What a contrast. The prophet didn't care, but a group of pagan sailors did. One man refused to fear the Lord, but a whole group of outsiders gained a new fear that led them into worship. Fortunately for Jonah, God is not through with him yet. Rebelling even to the point of death, God still pursues him.

Truth be told, Jonah had a choice to make. He was either going to do this God's way or his own way, and he chose the latter. And where did he end up? In the belly of a fish.

"And the Lord appointed a great fish to swallow up Jonah. And Jonah was in the belly of the fish three days and three nights" (v. 17 ESV).

Now, look at that verse closely. What sticks out to you? Of course we look at the miraculous—a fish swallowing a man and the man being able to survive in his belly for three days and three nights. But what else do you see? How about the words *"the Lord appointed"*? Imagine the feeling of being tossed over the side of a ship in the middle of a fierce storm. Once again, Jonah is going *down*, this time to the depths of the sea. But here again he finds God's grace, for "the Lord appointed a great fish" to swallow him.

First God *appointed* Jonah to be a prophet. He then *appointed* Jonah to go preach to the Ninevites. But Jonah went the other way. So God *appointed* a storm to intervene in the midst of Jonah's rebellion, and now he's *appointed* a great fish to be a part of the equation. The Sovereign God of the land and sea has boundless grace.

When it comes to God's plan for our lives, sometimes we have to come to the end of ourselves. And that is exactly where God allowed Jonah to go. He was at the end of his rope. He was at the bottom of *the ocean*, in the belly of a fish. You can't go anywhere but up from there.

Now imagine the darkness, the mucky-horrific-putrid place Jonah had to endure: a chewed-up fish, some rotten squid. . . . And this wasn't for just a couple of hours. This was for three days and three nights, which we know foreshadows the time Christ spent for us in the tomb.

So here's Jonah in complete darkness, and God is giving him a while to sort things out and experience the consequences of his own darkness. Three days' and three nights' worth. Though it's difficult to see the ones we love get to this place, sometimes it's what has to happen before there is a turnaround.

Finally, after Jonah attempts to run from God's presence, it's in the belly of a fish that he actually seeks his presence. We are told that "Jonah prayed to the Lord his God in the belly of the fish" (Jonah 2:1 ESV). It is a prayer of soberminded reality. He is in distress, on the doorsteps of death, which he knows he deserves. Yet he remembers God's character. He knows God's mercy. He believes in a God who answers prayer, and therefore he has hope. As Jonah writes this book, looking back on what he went through that day, this is what he says,

> I called out to the Lord, out of my distress, and he answered me; out of the belly of Sheol [the realm of the dead] I cried, and you heard my voice. For you cast me into the deep, into the heart of the seas, and the flood surrounded me; all your waves and your billows passed over me. Then I said, "I am driven away from your sight; yet I shall again look upon your holy temple." The waters closed in over me to take my life; the deep surrounded me; weeds were wrapped about my head at the roots of the mountains. I went down to the land whose bars closed upon me forever; yet you brought up my life from the pit, O Lord my God. When my life was fainting away, I remembered the Lord, and my prayer came to you, into your holy temple.
>
> vv. 2–7 ESV

Did you catch that Jonah said, "For *you* cast me into the deep"? Now wait a minute here. Who cast him into the sea? The sailors, right? But we see that Jonah recognizes God's sovereignty behind the free actions of sinful men—just like God sovereignly put Jesus on the cross through the actions of Pilate, the Romans, and the Jews. Humankind rebels, but God works all things for the good of those who are the "called" ones, those who know his salvation (see Romans 8:28).

Jonah also realized that even in the face of his impending death, there was always reason for hope because he knew he had a God who hears and answers prayer. His cry to God was heard, and the Lord brought his life back from "the pit." Though his life was fading away, God's plan was to rescue *him* from his rebellion before he could bring mercy to the Ninevites.

Jonah comes to his senses regarding his pride and says,

> Those who pay regard to vain idols forsake their hope of steadfast love. But I with the voice of thanksgiving will sacrifice to you; what I have vowed I will pay. Salvation belongs to the Lord!"

vv. 8–9 ESV

His pride, arrogance, and anger were the idols that invaded his life and took priority over God and his will. The NIV translation calls them "worthless idols." This is true for any pagan worshiper who worships real idols, or any God-fearing believer who allows the things of the world or the things of self to get in the way of their relationship with God.

Jonah knows better. Finally, he has a heart change (at least it looks that way at this point), and he gives thanks and worships the Lord with a vow, acknowledging that "salvation belongs to the Lord!" And at the Lord's command, the fish vomits Jonah onto the dry land.

Probably a little dazed but definitely grateful to be alive, Jonah is set free from his prison (the prison of the fish and the prison of his sin). God once again calls him to go preach to Nineveh. He hasn't told him what to say yet, but he commands him to go, for God often chooses to reveal his full will *as we obey him*, just like Abraham was to *go* to the land that God would soon show him.

So at the beginning of the book, we see that Jonah in his rebellion "rose to flee to Tarshish" (1:3 ESV). But this time we see Jonah "arose and went to Nineveh" (3:3 ESV). This time he obeys. And as he arrives he is given the message from the Lord that is clearly a *conditional promise* to the Ninevites: "Yet forty days, and Nineveh shall be overthrown!" (3:4 ESV).

The number *forty* is significant, for it is a number that has often been associated with judgment. You might remember when Noah built an ark, it rained for forty days and forty nights as God destroyed mankind and judged sin on the earth. The Israelites were in the desert for forty years because of their rebellion against God, and none of that generation, except two, entered the promised land. So "Forty days, and Nineveh shall be overthrown!" is a pretty serious warning.

But notice the command for the Ninevites to repent is somewhat *implied* in this. In forty days, Nineveh shall be overthrown . . . (*so . . . repent then?*). What baffles me is that Jonah doesn't tell them to repent. He doesn't offer forgiveness. He basically says, "You guys are going down."

I can't help but wonder if we are seeing more of Jonah's initial attitude here. Remember, he hated the Ninevites. So he probably had some secret joy in being able to say that Nineveh was about to be overthrown. Was his heart really changed if the idea of repentance was not explicit but merely implied? He's being obedient to God, but it doesn't seem like his heart has really changed. Nevertheless, God still uses sinners who are willing to speak for him. And to his credit, Jonah *is* speaking for God here. What happens next is perhaps the biggest miracle of the entire book: "And the people of Nineveh believed God. They called for a fast and put on sackcloth [a sign of repentance], from the greatest of them to the least of them" (3:5 ESV).

Jonah didn't tell them to repent, but the people of Nineveh did anyway. They heard God's word in the voice of Jonah. All Jonah had to do was open his mouth, and God's word did the rest, because there is inherent power in the Word of God. Don't worry about being a brilliant Bible teacher. Don't worry about having all the right answers and the best arguments. Just speak, and the Word of God does its own thing. But the miracle is not over. Watch this:

> The word reached the king of Nineveh, and he arose from his throne, removed his robe, covered himself with sackcloth, and sat in ashes. And he issued a proclamation and published through Nineveh, "By the decree of the king and his nobles: Let neither man nor beast, herd nor flock, taste anything. Let them not feed or drink water, but let man and beast be covered with sackcloth, and let them call out mightily to God. Let everyone turn from his evil way and from the violence that is in his hands. Who knows? God may turn and relent and turn from his fierce anger, so that we may not perish."
>
> 3:6–9 ESV

Amazingly, the king of Nineveh is so gripped by God's word through Jonah that he even calls for the animals to be draped in the sign of repentance. I don't know how you get a cow to repent, or why. Maybe they were producing skim milk, and it was time to be made whole again. (I couldn't resist.)

I think the king of Nineveh was trying to cover all his bases. The great king of this great city hears God's word, and the whole place is reduced to sackcloth and ashes.

They humbled themselves, abandoned their pride, gave up their evil ways, renounced violence, and repented on the spot. Now, that's a miracle wrought by the word of God! They were gripped by God's holiness while simultaneously seeing their sin. So they repented, which involves heartfelt sorrow for sin, a decision to renounce it, and a commitment to forsake it.[3] Then we are told this: "Then God saw their actions—that they had turned from their evil ways—so God relented from the disaster He had threatened to do to them. And He did not do it" (3:10).

Success. Ministry success today should never be measured by the size of the building or the crowd, but by the change in people's hearts and lives through the message of repentance and faith.

God's word through Jonah was powerful, and you would think Jonah would be thrilled to be a successful messenger of God, but that's not what we see.

But Jonah was greatly displeased and became furious. He prayed to the Lord: "Please, Lord, isn't this what I said while I was still in my own country? That's why I fled toward Tarshish in the first place. I knew that You are a merciful and compassionate God, slow to become angry, rich in faithful love, and One who relents from sending disaster. And now, Lord, please take my life from me, for it is better for me to die than to live."

4:1–3

So once again, Jonah would rather die! Does this make any sense? Now we're seeing the *real heart* of Jonah. He never wanted the Ninevites to repent in the first place. He wanted them to be judged. God was acting way outside the box here, and Jonah didn't like it. Why?

Because Jonah was prejudiced, self-absorbed, and self-deceived. He didn't seem to realize that he was not worthy of God's grace either. He was too puffed up for that. He took great pride in being a prophet of God. He loved his national heritage as an Israelite. In fact, go back and look at the very first words Jonah utters in this book: "He answered [the sailors], 'I'm a Hebrew . . .'" (Jonah 1:9).

I'm a Hebrew! See me? Hey, everyone, I'm a Hebrew. Jonah seemed to like his identity all too well. And the Ninevites are Assyrians, not Hebrews.

It seems like Jonah would have made a very good New Testament Pharisee. Proud of their religious status and who they were on the outside, but on the inside, they were someone else.

One of my favorite preachers, James MacDonald, tells the story of the boy who came into the classroom one day, and when the teacher told everyone to take a seat, the boy refused to do it. The teacher looked at the boy and said, "Please sit down." And the boy said, "No!"

The teacher said, "Young man, you sit down right now." And the boy again said, "No!" So the teacher walked over and pushed the kid down into his seat, forcing him to sit down. The young boy looked up and said, "I may be sitting on the outside, but on the inside I'm still standing up."

That was Jonah! Jonah didn't agree with how God was going about things. He may have agreed to go preach, but he still rebelled against God in his heart. Nothing had changed, and it makes you wonder what really happened to Jonah back in chapter 2, when he recited that wonderful prayer in the belly of a fish.

Crying out to God, seemingly coming to his senses, Jonah gives thanks, makes a vow, and rightly says that "salvation comes from the Lord" (2:9 NIV 1984). He is humbled and ready to do God's will. But then all of that seems to be a bunch of wish-wash—nothing more than lip service. True repentance and true belief bear fruit. Ironically, Jonah is a prophet, called to bring a message of repentance, but he refuses to repent himself. Jonah would rather die because God didn't meet his expectations. But God engages him: "The Lord asked, 'Is it right for you to be angry?'" (4:4).

Jonah doesn't respond. He merely walks away and isolates himself. When people are mad and disillusioned with God, they have a tendency to distance themselves. Jonah takes his ball and goes home, so to speak. He leaves the city, makes himself a shelter, and sits down, to no avail, waiting to see if by some chance the city will be judged.

But God's grace to Jonah is still abundant. The Lord *appoints* a plant to grow overnight to be a shade for Jonah's head, which temporarily makes him happy. But then the Lord *appoints* a worm to chew up the vine so that it withers. The sun pounds down on Jonah, and he asks yet again to die.

Again God asks him what right he has to be angry, and Jonah says he is angry enough to die.

> So the Lord said, "You cared about the plant, which you did not labor over and did not grow. It appeared in a night and perished in a night. Should I not care about the great city of Nineveh, which has more than 120,000 people who cannot distinguish between their right and their left, as well as many animals?"

4:10–11

Notice the last words: "as well as many animals." It's as if God is saying, "Jonah, I am a God of grace. I care about everything I have made. Even the Ninevites. Even the animals. And I will have mercy upon whom I will have mercy." (See also Romans 9:15.)

God gives grace time and again to people who don't deserve it. Thank you, Lord, for apart from that grace we would all be nothing.

That's where the book of Jonah ends. There is no Jonah 5. And we are left with a Jonah, who is seemingly unreconciled to God. But remember, this story is not about Jonah.

It's about the unending mercy and grace of God, a God who pursues us. It's about a God who sovereignly orchestrates, appoints, and works out the details of his people's lives—the lives of those who make willing choices, choices that God can still use for his glory and our good no matter how bad they may be.

So ask yourself this: Is my life about me? Is it about my comfort? Have I placed God in a box so that when he gets "out of line" I have a tendency to get mad and withdraw and walk away? Or do I fall down before him, and with all of my being worship him and surrender and say, "You are an awesome God! You are a gracious and merciful God, slow to anger and abounding in steadfast love."

This is not your average fish story—because in the end, it's not about a fish at all. It's not about Jonah either. It's all about God.

5

The Woman Caught in Adultery

"Go, and from now on do not sin anymore."

—John 8:11

I f there is one thing sinful human beings are really good at, it's rationalizing sin. Take, for example, that chocolate muffin sitting before you. Perhaps you think a Diet Coke or a skinny latte may cancel out the calories in that muffin. Not so fast. Sure, I'm being a little silly, but when it comes to people trying to get away with something, we can manufacture the best excuses—in fact, we've become experts at it. We are kings and queens of rationalization.

We even go as far as blaming others for our shortcomings. When Adam sinned in the garden of Eden, he first blamed God and then Eve for his own sin. He was quick to "toss someone else under the bus" before he was willing to admit he was responsible for disobeying God. And when it comes to our sin, we by nature can be very defensive in order to avoid shame.

It is a fact that we are all sinners. Paul reminds us in Romans, "For *all* have sinned and fall short of the glory of God" (3:23). Therefore, the playing field is quite level. But it is another thing to say "we're all sinners" in an attempt to dismiss or avoid any responsibility for our sin, which some often do.

If we are confronted by our sin, it is not an acceptable excuse to blame someone else, pull out the "nobody's perfect" card, or even to explain things away by stating, "I'm only human."[1] All of those sin-dodging techniques don't deal with the reality that we are stained with sinful hearts that need forgiveness and grace. We are still on the hook.

Unfortunately, a popular Bible story has also been used as a shield for sin. It stems from the gospel of John, chapter eight.[2] It is an uncomfortable story to be sure, for it begins with a woman who has been "caught in the act of adultery" (8:4 ESV). No further details are given, and perhaps that is for the best. The scribes and Pharisees bring her to Jesus and place her in the center of their circle. They question Jesus about what should happen to her, since the Old Testament law of Moses says such a person should be stoned (Leviticus 20:10; Deuteronomy 22:23–24). This may seem overly harsh, but it was the law for the nation of Israel, as God wanted his people to be pure and separated from the pagan practices of the Canaanites.[3]

But Jesus knew the motives of the scribes and Pharisees were tainted. They weren't really interested in true justice according to the law. Otherwise, they would have brought the man too. John himself even says, "They asked this to trap Him [Jesus], in order that they might have evidence to accuse Him" (John 8:6).

Accuse Jesus of what? Anything. They wanted to get Jesus in trouble. They thought that if Jesus said no to the stoning, he would be guilty of violating the law of Moses. Yet if Jesus agreed and insisted on the stoning, they would have him pitted against the local Roman law, for the Romans zealously guarded their laws that claimed they alone had sole authority to carry out the death penalty. In either situation, they thought they had Jesus pinned down.

So they weren't after the woman, guilty as she might be. They were really after Jesus. But there is good news for the woman because they brought her to Jesus. The Old Testament law was weak in that it brought a lot of guilt but offered little or no grace; but that was all to change with the coming of Jesus—the man whom John said was "full of grace and truth" (1:14).

In what is the only recorded moment of Jesus' writing, he bends down and scrawls something in the sand with his finger. We don't know what he wrote, and it would be mere speculation to guess, but it certainly raised the dramatic tension of the scene. Perhaps they thought Jesus was stalling, so they persisted and pressed him to give them an answer.

Jesus' response was brilliant. He didn't refute the Old Testament law, nor did he excuse the woman's sin. And he didn't set himself against the laws of the Romans either. He replied, "He who is without sin among you, let him cast the first stone at her" (John 8:7, author's paraphrase). Then Jesus bent down again and wrote some more.

If the words on the ground were not their written indictment, then Jesus' own words to them certainly had to be. One by one, starting with the old men first, the scribes and Pharisees began to walk away. These graceless men were faced with the reality that they too needed grace, and Jesus had stolen their thunder. They had nothing more to say, as if Jesus had just robbed them of their ammunition.

Ironically, Jesus called them out on the motives they had for an even greater sin. In their zeal to condemn this woman, they failed to see that their desire to put Jesus (a sinless man) to death would be the greater sin. But they weren't interested in being confronted about their own past or present sins, and so the scene clears until it is Jesus and the woman alone.

But here is where many people forget to read the rest of the story. Some will simply stop here and say, "See, we're all sinners, so no one has the right to judge me or hold me (or anyone else) accountable." And in thinking or saying that, they would be outright wrong.

It is true the woman needed grace, but she needed a dose of truth as well. Again, she is standing before the right person, the man of grace and truth. Jesus first asks the woman if there is anyone left to accuse her, and she replies, "No one, Lord."

Notice this. She calls Jesus Lord. That's a positive sign. She recognizes his authority over her. In the end, this previews what all of us will have to experience—standing before the Lord as sinners in need of his grace. And grace is what she received. The accusers that sought to condemn her to death were gone; there was no one left to do it.

And in a moment of profound mercy, Jesus himself states, "I do not condemn you either" (NASB). Now was not the time of condemnation, now was the season of grace. Now was the time for the Lord's mercy ("the year of the Lord's favor"—Luke 4:19). His first coming was all about salvation from sin, whereas his second coming would be about the judgment of sin—judgment for those who refused to repent and believe in him.

But even though Jesus did not condemn her, neither did he acquit her. He demanded repentance. If she was to receive forgiveness, she would need to repent, and to demonstrate that repentance is part of an ongoing life of obedience. Therefore, Jesus emphatically says, "Go, and from now on sin no more" (ESV).

There it is—words that do not allow anyone to live behind a shield so they can go on sinning. Actually, they are words of life, another opportunity to live free from the bondage of sin. But they require something of us as well. We all have to come to terms with the fact that we are sinners, but we cannot use that thought as a way to excuse ourselves or dismiss ourselves from accountability and responsibility for it. Rather, the fact that we are sinners should drive us toward a weighty and personally felt need for grace.

People don't often realize it, but conviction of sin is actually part of God's gift to us. It may not feel like a gift. It may make us feel awful at first, but it is part of the process God takes us through to deliver us from bondage while bringing us into the freedom of his grace. On the other side of it, the Holy Spirit that convicted us is the same Spirit that delivers us and washes us clean, bringing us refreshing joy. Jesus died not only to pardon our sins but to deliver us *from* them as well.

It is so easy to rationalize, to blame someone else, or to find an excuse for our sins so that we don't have to answer for them. But the fact remains, we will all have to face judgment at some point.

The good news is that when we repent and turn from a life of sin and turn our hearts in faith toward Jesus, we receive forgiveness, mercy, and grace before the throne of God. Paul said, "There is therefore now no condemnation for those who are in Christ Jesus" (Romans 8:1 ESV). When God became a man, lived a perfect life, and was condemned to the cross, our sins were placed on him, and his grace was mercifully credited to us. The great reformer Martin Luther called this "the great exchange." God took my sin and yours and exchanged it for his grace.

Hiding behind excuses does nothing for us, but hiding behind the cross gives us all that we need. Therefore, keeping people at arm's length by saying "He who is without sin cast the first stone" is misusing the verse for a purpose it was never intended to have. Perhaps what we should remember from this story are the last words of Jesus: "Neither do I condemn you. . . . Go, and from now on do not sin anymore."

6

Jesus Could Not Do Miracles in His Hometown

And He was amazed at their unbelief.

—Mark 6:6

Many of us have had the experience of moving away from where we grew up only to come back for a visit and be stunned by all the changes that have taken place. Maybe a new gas station has been erected, the makeshift baseball diamond you played on is now a parking lot, and trees you climbed as a kid have been cut down. Furthermore, everything seems smaller than it did when you were young.

Yet in the midst of all the aesthetic changes, some things never change. The apple orchard still has the best cider for sale. The people you've always known still seem the same to you—just a little older. Their smiles, their laughs, and their jokes are no different from what you remember. It feels like home.

I wonder what it was like for Jesus when he finally went back home to Nazareth, where he had been raised.

Joseph and Mary's oldest is back—the carpenter's son who was such a good boy all the time, never getting into trouble. And a lot has happened since he left; not so much with Nazareth, but with him. Rumor has it he's been doing extraordinary miracles. He teaches with amazing authority. Crowds are following him. His popularity is unprecedented.

What kind of reception would Jesus receive?

We find out in the gospel accounts, and for our purposes we will look at Mark's brief account of Jesus' time in Nazareth, including a section of Scripture that some twist regarding physical healing and its relationship to one's measure of faith.

Mark 6 begins with Jesus continuing his teaching ministry, this time in his hometown synagogue. It was the Sabbath, and his teaching was full of the Holy Spirit's power and carried a measure of outright authority to it. The people were amazed. Surprised, actually. Their questions were understandable: "'Where did this man get these things?' they said. 'What is this wisdom given to Him, and how are these miracles performed by His hands?'" (Mark 6:2).

He was not the same man they knew when he left. Something had happened. One thing was for sure, they recognized him in one sense. They knew his family: "Isn't this the carpenter, the son of Mary, and the brother of James, Joses, Judas, and Simon? And aren't His sisters here with us?" (6:3).

Despite what some teach, Jesus was not an only child. He was the first child Mary had, but after his miraculous birth, Mary and Joseph had other children, some of them even listed in the text. They were technically his half brothers and sisters. And apparently Joseph had already passed away at this point, since he is not listed along with the family. The people now knew Jesus as the "son of Mary," the only place in Scripture where he is called this.

In their minds, they could not conceive of where he had received such authority and giftedness. After all, he had a commoner's trade. They only knew him as a carpenter, someone who carved wood and stone. *Who does he think he is?* they may have thought. The text says they "took offense" (ESV) or "were offended" by him (v. 3).

There seem to be two kinds of local reactions that surface when someone from a small town becomes famous or makes a name for himself: Either they celebrate and take pride in the fact that one of their own has received the blessing of God (little did they know, in Jesus' case), or they tend to be jealous, skeptical, and bent on keeping that person humble by making it their personal mission to keep him or her down to earth so they don't get a big head.

With Jesus, it seems the latter was the people's response. In fact, it may have been even worse than that. To be offended by his teaching on faith and the kingdom represents an even deeper resentment and faithlessness, not only toward him but toward the things of God. Unfortunately, this was not something new. This kind of reaction had historical precedent.

For years the prophets of old in Israel's history suffered persecution and even death because God's people did not take an interest in what they had to say. They didn't take kindly to the fact that they were being called out on their sin. The prophet Jeremiah was beaten, put in stocks, and even thrown into a cistern at one point. Tradition holds that Isaiah was actually sawn in two. So the job description of a prophet was not one that endeared the man to the people, and Jesus clearly pointed this out next when he said, "A prophet is not without honor except in his hometown, among his relatives, and in his household" (Mark 6:4).

Truly Jesus was a prophet, receiving a prophet's reception. But even so, he was much more than a prophet. He was the Messiah. But the people familiar with him in his hometown had little tolerance for such a thought and absolutely no faith to believe it. To them he was scandalous, and in the gospel of Luke it says they ended up nearly running him off of a cliff. But not today.

However, Mark tells us something very peculiar that many have misunderstood and misused when it comes to healing and faith: "[Jesus] was not able to do any miracles there, except that He laid His hands on a few sick people and healed them. And He was amazed at their unbelief" (Mark 6:5–6).

"Was not able" (or "he could not do") is an interesting phrase, to say the least. The text says Jesus could not do any miracles there except for a few healings. This gives the impression that Jesus was unable to use his supernatural power because there was such widespread unbelief. But I assert that it wasn't as though the unbelief of the people had more power over the situation than he did. Jesus had complete authority over nature and could do miracles of all kinds by the word of his mouth.

65

In other words, their unbelief was not some kind of cosmic kryptonite that weakened Jesus' abilities to perform miracles as the Messiah. Rather, it seems that Jesus limited his expression of divine authority as a form of judgment on their rejection of him. Sometimes the withholding of certain blessings is a form of God's discipline or judgment.

It was not that he could not heal; he merely chose not to. Further, it is not likely that many of them were coming to be healed in the first place, since they merely called him the carpenter. Either way, the healings were few because of their unbelief.

But the question is, is this always the case when it comes to God's decision to heal or not to heal? Is it always dependent on whether or not we have enough faith? I would say no. Some teach that healing is *always* contingent on the measure of our faith, and if healing doesn't come, the only conclusion is that the petitioner may not have enough faith; and they appeal to this passage in Mark as their proof text.

This line of thinking is a half-truth, and it has caused an immeasurable amount of grief for some true believers who have been sold this lie as an answer for why their loved one did not survive a debilitating illness or a terminal disease. Once believed, this half-truth can bring on crippling guilt and a belief that God is punishing the one without "enough faith." It can result in resentment and bitterness toward God, the church, or even toward the one who has prayed.

Many a suffering soul has left the church and walked away from God because they were somehow convinced that the death of their loved one was their own fault—as if God could not do a miracle because it was contingent on an unknown measure of faith.

But there is something dead wrong about that line of teaching and thinking, and we need only to look at the full counsel of the Word of God—all of what the Bible teaches—to put things in their proper order.

First, within a half-truth there is always a hint of truth. And that truth is this: Jesus does respond to faith. In fact, so many miracles that he did choose to perform are seen in connection with Jesus' asking for and commending the people for their faith. We can't avoid the fact that his power to heal is certainly connected to the faith of the individual. In Matthew 9, for example, Jesus healed two blind men and said, "According to your faith it will be done to you" (v. 29, author's paraphrase). In another example, when the apostle Paul entered Lystra, he came upon a crippled man who was lame from birth and who took an interest in what Paul was preaching. The Bible says, "Paul, looking intently at him and seeing that he had faith to be made well, said in a loud voice, 'Stand upright on your feet.' And he sprang up and began walking" (Acts 14:9–10 ESV).

So it is an obvious conclusion that a biblical view of healing includes the importance and, at times, the necessity of faith in order to bring about the desired results. And it would seem that in the case of Jesus' performing miracles in his hometown, it was truly their lack of faith that caused Jesus to restrain his miracle-working power.

But having said all that, it is quite another thing to teach that in *all cases* where healing does not take place it is due to the fact that there was no faith, little faith, or not enough faith to manipulate God's hand of favor. That conclusion is not warranted when we look at the entire teaching of the Bible.

In fact, one of the best examples of this comes from the apostle Paul, who, as many might argue, was perhaps the most dynamic Christian to ever live. He was certainly a great leader and shepherd of God's people, an outstanding evangelist, and a first-rate mentor who knew how to disciple people. But he wasn't perfect. He had weaknesses that he would readily admit to (Romans 7), and in humility he once called himself the worst of sinners (1 Timothy 1:15). But few would argue that Paul didn't have adequate faith. In fact, he set the standard for faith. Yet even in the midst of this apostle's walk with God, there was an area that caused him great grief and pain.

Many have speculated about what it might have been. Was it pride, an outside opponent, or some kind of physical issue (or maybe all of the above)? Either way, Paul talks about it in 2 Corinthians. In the context of the passage, Paul discusses the revelations from God that he has received in the past as an apostle. These visions and revelations from the Lord brought him to the point where he was even able to get a glimpse of heaven itself (something very few in Scripture were able to see).

Paul then says that in order to keep him from becoming conceited to the point of exalting himself, there was given to him a "thorn in his flesh," something to keep him humble. The key to interpretation may be in the text itself: "Therefore, so that I would not exalt myself, a thorn in the flesh was given to me, a messenger of Satan to torment me so I would not exalt myself" (2 Corinthians 12:7).

Note a couple of things: First, Paul said this thorn was given to him, which means it came from God purposefully to keep him humble and dependent upon God. Whereas oftentimes we plead with God, just like Paul did, to take things away (more on that in a minute), our suffering may have been given or allowed for God's purposes that reach far beyond the scope of our imagination. Such was the case with Job's difficulties in life.

Second, the nature of the thorn may not have been physical but spiritual in nature. For Paul calls it a "messenger [or angel] of Satan," sent to torment him. This suggests it may have something to do with the demonic, perhaps even the deceptive teachings of false teachers whom he constantly battled and who were seeking to lead the church astray by the "teachings of demons" (1 Timothy 4:1). They could be considered a thorn in his flesh, requiring him to defend the gospel or his own reputation as an apostle, or perhaps to spend hours in desperate prayer for the church to be protected.

No matter what the reason, even though it was uncomfortable and agonizing for Paul, this thorn caused him to be even more dependent upon the Lord.

> Concerning this, I pleaded with the Lord three times to take it away from me. But He said to me, "My grace is sufficient for you, for power is perfected in weakness."
>
> 2 Corinthians 12:8–9

Few would argue that Paul was deficient in faith and because of his lack of faith he was unable to be rid of this problem. Here we have a man who, next to Abraham, may have been the greatest example of faith we have ever seen. For Paul, relief did not come because of the amount of faith he did or didn't have. Rather, it was because healing *was not a part of God's ultimate purpose* for him.

So healing isn't always contingent on the amount of our faith. It is true that faith is the means by which God often heals, but there are times when healing will not come because God has other plans. This is where we must pray in faith, believe that God can do it, and leave the results to him, trusting in his sovereign plan.

Paul received the blessing of "sufficient grace," something that is often not as appreciated as it should be. Grace is God's gift, and sufficient grace is a gift that enables us to carry on for as long as God needs us to. It further requires us to wean ourselves from our tendency to be self-sufficient, and to trust in the strength that only God provides. This is why Paul said,

> Therefore, I will most gladly boast all the more about my weaknesses, so that Christ's power may reside in me. So I take pleasure in weaknesses, insults, catastrophes, persecutions, and in pressures, because of Christ. For when I am weak, then I am strong.
>
> vv. 9–10

Paul knew that his weakness gave God's strength a platform to be put on display, so that in the end God's power and might would receive the ultimate praise and glory.

So when it comes to the story of Jesus' hometown or the story of Paul's thorn, there are some conclusions that we must come to by looking at both stories in harmony with each other.

First, it is true that sometimes God will withhold healing because of a lack of faith as a form of judgment on unbelief. This was true for the time Jesus entered his hometown, where faith was obviously missing. *But this does not mean that every time healing does not come it is always due to a lack of faith*, which is what we learn from Paul's experience, because Paul certainly was a man of faith.

Second, Paul's experience also teaches us that though it is true that God does look for faith and will heal in response to faith, sometimes his decision to heal or not to heal may not be related to our faith at all, but may be in accordance with his sovereign purposes for us. He may be looking for a platform to display his sufficient grace.

I am a firm believer in this latter idea, especially when it comes to Christians who are in the process of dying. Though it is perfectly right and God-glorifying to pray for healing for a brother or sister in Christ, sometimes it is God's will to call that person home to glory, and he will give them sufficient grace to endure all the way to the end. In fact, the journey may be one of the greatest opportunities to witness and display faith to those who are seeing it happen.

You might not realize it, but your pathway home (the process of a Christian's death) may be one of the most remarkable times in your life to glorify God by putting your faith in his gospel on display—trusting in his saving hand to bring you to glory.

It is here that our witness may have the greatest impact on others—and in this sense we can be happy that God is not healing us for further life on earth but rather preparing us for ultimate healing in the life to come, giving us an opportunity to impact others and share our faith on our journey there.

Either way, for the Christian, God will heal—in this life or in the life to come. We must live by faith and not by sight. If he heals us here, then great! That may mean more fruitful labor for Christ while in the body. But if he doesn't heal us, then let us rejoice in the grace he gives that is being put on display, and let us rejoice in the plan he has to call us home to be healed once and for all. And let us not assume that someone's healing or lack of it is *always* contingent upon faith, because we don't always see things from God's perspective. And we can't speak for God in those situations.

7

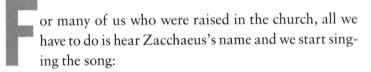

Zacchaeus

"Zacchaeus, hurry and come down, for I must
stay at your house today."

—Luke 19:5 ESV

For many of us who were raised in the church, all we
have to do is hear Zacchaeus's name and we start singing the song:

> Zacchaeus was a wee little man and a wee little man
>   was he.
> He climbed up in a sycamore tree for the Lord he
>   wanted to see.
> And as the Savior passed that way He looked up in
>   the tree.
> And He said, "Zacchaeus, you come down,
> for I'm going to your house today,
> for I'm going to your house today."

The song is still popular today in many local children's ministries, summer Bible schools, church camps, and so on. It is a catchy tune about an unlikely encounter between Jesus and one of the most despised men of his time, a Jewish tax collector. But the story, found only in the gospel of Luke, has often been misunderstood in at least two different ways, leading many to misplace the emphasis of the story and miss the beauty of it altogether.

We find the story in Luke 19, and Jesus has just delivered and healed a man named Bartimaeus from his *physical* blindness and *poverty*. But as Jesus enters the city of Jericho, he is going to encounter another man who ironically needs to be delivered from his *spiritual* blindness and *wealth*, a man so despised by the community that they would have likely referred to him as a traitor.

Why such a harsh label? It wasn't merely because they didn't like paying taxes, but because of the one they were forced to pay their taxes to—the collector—and the unjust amount that was required.

The Jews viewed the pagan Romans as the oppressive oc-cupying force that had invaded and taken captive their land. And like the Greeks before them, they introduced all kinds of idolatry and immorality to the geography, culture, and people of Israel. This is why most of the Jews in Jesus' day hoped the Messiah would come as a military ruler who would *im-mediately* deliver them from their enemies.[1] Paying tribute and taxes to the Romans went against the very fiber of their deepest convictions, and they were waiting for deliverance. In their eyes, tax collectors by nature were a reminder of this oppression.

Second, as if paying taxes to Rome and the Emperor wasn't bad enough, even worse was seeing a *Jewish man* working for the Roman government, which was the case of many of the tax collectors. This was tantamount to treason in their eyes—someone who worked for the oppressor and who seemingly had no problem preying on his own people for the cause of the enemy and for the sake of personal profit.

Indeed, there was much profit to be found. Many of the tax collectors were known for overcharging or collecting more than was required, simply for personal gain, while using the full authority of their office to do it. This was something Rome seemingly turned a blind eye toward, and the tax collectors were notoriously wealthy because of it. Further, Luke tells us that Zacchaeus was a chief tax collector, who likely was in charge of many other collectors in the wealthy, prosperous trading tax district of Jericho.

So Zacchaeus would have been seen as an archenemy—a wealthy traitor who worked for the most despised of all people. This is why his encounter with Jesus is gripping to say the least, because the extent of God's saving power is on full display. There is no one who is beyond the grace of Jesus, for our pursuing God knows how to turn an enemy into a friend and to turn the lost into the found.

The story unfolds with Jesus entering Jericho, a historic city in the Jordan Valley that was later rebuilt after Joshua's conquest.[2] Interestingly, during its original destruction by Joshua and the Israelites, the command was to utterly destroy everything in the city except for certain treasures that were to be dedicated to the treasury of the Lord. Yet one individual named Achan disobeyed that instruction and claimed some of the forbidden treasure for himself, thus bringing disfavor from the Lord on the armies of Israel, who were defeated in subsequent battles until Achan's sin was exposed.

So this city of Jericho has an interesting connection to thievery and deception, and the master thief in the Jericho of Jesus' day was likely this tax collector named Zacchaeus. Luke tells us Jesus was "passing through," but surely he had more in mind than that.

On his way through town, Luke describes Zacchaeus as a curious fellow. Perhaps it was the crowds with Jesus that garnered his attention. Perhaps he'd heard of Jesus from an earlier account by his colleagues of how one tax collector named Levi (later renamed Matthew the disciple) left his post to follow him, and therefore he was curious about who this Jesus was (see Luke 5:27–32).

The fact is we are not told why Zacchaeus is interested in seeing Jesus. One commentator suggests that "he had a dissatisfied heart," that he "knew he was alienated from God . . . lacked eternal life . . ." and was "feeling guilty about his sin."[3] This is certainly likely, and would make sense due to the fact that his particular sin would cause him to feel alienation not only before God but also with his fellow man.

Biblically speaking, we know that true saving faith necessitates the presence of genuine repentance, so we can safely assume that God was already working in his heart as Jesus approached.

Of all the things that Zacchaeus could be accused of, no one could accuse him of lacking in the areas of creativity and resourcefulness. Luke tells us,

[Zacchaeus] was trying to see who Jesus was, but he was not able because of the crowd, since he was a short man. So running ahead, he climbed up a sycamore tree to see Jesus, since He was about to pass that way.

19:3–4

I happen to be six-foot, six-inches tall, so for me, seeing at parades and large-scale events is never really a problem. Women in the supermarket often stop me to ask if I can reach that product on the top shelf for them. *"No problem, ma'am."* But Zacchaeus was just the opposite: vertically challenged. And he was no dummy.

After scoping the grounds, he locates a sycamore-fig tree. This is not the kind of sycamore trees we have in North America that are tall with big leaves, white bark, and grow near water. The type of tree referenced here grows in the Jordan Valley and has branches that grow near the ground. "The fruit looks like a fig, but the taste is unpleasant. It is eaten by the poor."[4]

The fact that Zacchaeus would scale a tree that primarily fed the poor seems ironic since many of the people around Jericho were poor because of Zacchaeus. And the fruit of Zacchaeus's life up until this point was rather unpleasant as well, but that was all about to change. He scaled the tree to get a better view.

> When Jesus came to the place, He looked up and said to him, "Zacchaeus, hurry and come down because today I must stay at your house." So he quickly came down and welcomed Him joyfully. All who saw it began to complain, "He's gone to lodge with a sinful man!"
>
> Luke 19:5–7

Several things here should astonish us. This is vintage Jesus. Nothing he does is random but is rather purposeful.

Of all the people there that day, Jesus stopped to take notice of one man perched in a tree—but not just any man, a rather isolated man. A wealthy man, mind you, but a guilty man nonetheless. Perhaps he was a man under conviction as well. Jesus knew the heart, and he knew more than that.

In what surely must have caused Zacchaeus's heart to skip a beat, Jesus stops to look directly at him, and calls him out *by name*. But how could he have known? We have no indication that these two had ever met before. But here we have further evidence that as God in the flesh, Jesus knows things and does things that only God can know or do.

Drawing on his divine omniscience, Jesus addresses Zacchaeus in no uncertain terms. He commands the tax collector to come down from his elevated position and to do it with haste. Jesus has an agenda and says, "Today I *must* stay at your house." In other words, Jesus invites himself in, and Zacchaeus joyfully and willingly accepts.

Such is the case when a man or woman comes to faith. Jesus takes the initiative, and the heart has a willing response.

Without delay, the tax collector collects himself, descends from his advantageous position, and welcomes Jesus into his most intimate of places, his life and his home. For the first time in his life, he feels the stigma of his sin washed away.

Interestingly, the wrath of human scorn moves away from the tax collector toward the Savior as those who are watching complain and say, "He's gone to lodge with a sinful man!" Indeed, Jesus has a way of taking wrath away from believing sinners and absorbing it himself.

But this didn't bother Jesus or Zacchaeus, as there was too much joy to be had. Jesus crossed all religious and social barriers to have close, personal fellowship with an "unclean" man who was in need of God's love and grace. Later, the apostle Paul would echo a similar idea when he wrote, "But God proves His own love for us in that while we were still sinners, Christ died for us!" (Romans 5:8).

We have a God who left the comforts of heaven to submit himself to a disgrace that only we deserved—death on a cross. Even while we were sinners, even when we were designated as enemies (Romans 5:10), Christ did the unexpected, and we as the undeserving are radically changed and transformed when through faith we come face-to-face with this kind of redeeming love.

Apparently this was the case with Zacchaeus. Though we do not have the full inside conversation between the Savior and the tax collector, we can definitely see the results. The fruit of Zacchaeus's life took on an instant change—he immediately bore the fruit of repentance.

> But Zacchaeus stood there and said to the Lord, "Look, I'll give half of my possessions to the poor, Lord! And if I have extorted anything from anyone, I'll pay back four times as much!"
>
> Luke 19:8

Everybody knew what Zacchaeus's sin was, and Zacchaeus himself was willing to publicly confess it. Further, he declared that half his possessions would be given to the poor and that if he had defrauded or extorted money from anyone, he would pay them back fourfold and make restitution for the wrong committed.

It's a beautiful thing to see the weight of sin fall off someone, but that can only come through genuine repentance. And those who have truly repented are fully aware of the priceless blessing that God's forgiveness is—a forgiveness that removes the weight of guilt and shame. This freeing feeling was now Zacchaeus's to enjoy. He was a slave to money no more.

And the words of Jesus confirmed the reality of this spiritual freedom: "Today salvation has come to this house," Jesus told him, "because he too is a son of Abraham" (Luke 19:9).

The words of Christ here deserve some close examination. First, Jesus said, "*Today* salvation has come to this house," referring obviously to Zacchaeus. This should refute any confusion about the timing of Zacchaeus's conversion. Yesterday he was not saved, but today he is.

This stands in direct contrast to some recent speculation by scholars that Zacchaeus was a generous man of virtue who was already actively giving his money to the poor, such that Jesus was merely correcting a public misunderstanding about him.[5] This sort of reading of the text is not in keeping with Luke's overall purpose in this gospel: to show the extent of Christ's redeeming love to the underprivileged, overlooked, despised, and rejected (the tax collectors, lepers, Samaritans, children, the poor, and other underdogs of his day).

If Zacchaeus were already giving his money away and helping the poor, then surely his reputation would have been talked about positively by the people on the street. For news would travel fast if a tax collector were giving money away. But in this narrative, he is despised, and people were calling him a "sinful man." This surely suggests that this account is all about his conversion and not merely a public exoneration of a misunderstanding about him.

Further, Zacchaeus is called a "son of Abraham." Now, technically, he already was a physical descendant of Abraham, since he was a Jew. But Jesus is not using that idea here. Jesus is highlighting the man's faith, the same faith exercised by Abraham in the Old Testament, which saved him. This is what made him a "son."[6] Paul said something similar in Romans 2, when he said that a true Jew is not merely one who conforms to outward ethnicity, but rather a true Jew is one who conforms inwardly through faith. (See Romans 2:28–29.)

The fact that Jesus proclaims *today* as the day of salvation and that Zacchaeus is a son (in the truest sense) suggests a genuine conversion has just taken place and Jesus is teaching the people what true sonship looks like. Genuine repentance and saving faith bears fruit in a very public way.

But there is another way this story has often been misunderstood. Many think that Zacchaeus is the preeminent and model seeker, a man who is hungry for God and spiritual truth, who is so desperate to find it that he's willing to make a fool of himself by climbing a tree just to get the attention of a famous rabbi.

Though it is true that Zacchaeus has a genuine interest in seeing Jesus and may have indeed felt the guilt and alienation of his sin, it would be a mistake to conclude that the thrust of this story is about Zacchaeus seeking Jesus. Rather, it is the other way around.

Luke gives us the most poignant words of Jesus *as the main point of the story* in the very last verse: "For the Son of Man has come to seek and to save the lost" (Luke 19:10).

This is about Jesus seeking Zacchaeus. This is about a purposeful display of amazing grace in the most public sense. We have a God who delights in exhibiting his far-reaching grace to the most undeserving of sinners, people like you and me. Again, no one is beyond the scope of God's redeeming love.

He came to earth to seek and to save. This is what makes his grace so amazing. Even while we were sinners. Even while we were enemies. Even in our rebellion Jesus pursues us. He seeks in order to save, and this is precisely what he did on this day to one of the most hated people in that culture.

Just like the famous hymn says, "I once was lost, but now am found." We are the found ones. Why? Because God was pursuing us, seeking us. It's not as if we were pursuing him. For "there is no one righteous, not even one. There is no one who understands; there is no one who seeks God" (Romans 3:10–11). How humbling to have a God who does not give up on us, who chases us down with reconciling love. Do we do the same toward others? Jesus has given us an example to follow.

We might see Zacchaeus as a "wee little man," but Jesus made him into a spiritual giant. Jesus saw a perfect opportunity to make a public spectacle of his grace in vivid contrast to the self-righteous attitudes of the scribes and Pharisees who knew nothing of such grace. Zacchaeus may have been small in stature, but the salvation he received that day was larger than life.

8

Sowing Your Seed

"They are prophets of destruction, these are New
Age heretics saying they'll show the way to salvation, but their cross is a bloodless stick."

—Steve Camp, "The Agony of Deceit"

They are sly, sneaky, and crafty. They wear a mask and
may look attractive on the outside, but inside, they
are full of mischief. They seemingly have no fear and
they love darkness. You might think I am talking about rac-
coons—those clever mask-wearing creatures that are master
scavengers, prowling in the night.

But truth be told, I am talking about the spiritually bank-
rupt but materially wealthy con artists known as prosperity-
gospel preachers. They are sly, sneaky, and crafty. They wear

83

masks, like a wolf in sheep's clothing. They are fearless, bold, and very good at what they do. Their hearts are full of darkness with a seared conscience, readily taking what doesn't belong to them.

One of the cruelest schemes to come out of the United States is the "prosperity gospel." This is the belief that God has plans for you in the here and now to receive all the health and wealth you deserve in response to the measure of your own giving and faith.

Prosperity preachers serve up a banquet of spiritual bunk at the expense of the weak, vulnerable, and desperate. They pad their own pockets by pulling the emotional heartstrings of those who want the American dream, with a spiritualized twist, calling you to give to their ministry so that a miracle of sizable proportion will come your way. (More on this in a minute.)

One might argue that the prosperity gospel has done more harm to the church of today than many other scandals, shortcomings, or cultural compromises. It is a deep perversion of the true gospel. What is the true gospel? It is the teaching of Jesus and the apostles that true spiritual life comes only through repentance from sin and faith in the life, death, and resurrection of Jesus Christ. And for the one who believes in this true gospel, a life of obedience and faith shows itself in denying oneself, taking up your cross daily, and following Jesus.

But you won't find that line of thinking in prosperity theology. In a helpful and riveting interview, prominent author, pastor, and teacher Dr. John Piper sets forth six keys to detecting the prosperity gospel and its preachers. He summarizes them as follows:[1]

"the absence of a doctrine of suffering"

"the absence of a clear and prominent doctrine of self-denial"

"the absence of serious exposition of Scripture"

"the absence of dealing with tensions in Scripture" [in other words, a willingness to teach something made up by the preacher that the Bible elsewhere would clearly contradict]

the preacher's own participation in an exorbitant lifestyle, where he lives above the average person in his parish

the exaltation of "self" and a marginalization of the greatness of God

One of the greatest needs in the church today is the spiritual discipline of discernment.[2] The church has become vulnerable to the persuasive messages of prosperity theology due to the fact that many churches no longer teach a gospel-centered, biblically based theology from the pulpit. Much of what is taught today could be categorized as man-centered, therapeutic, and entertainment driven.

Tragically, the measure of a church's success is often rated in human terms, such as size, scope, sales, and marketing. This focus on externals has robbed the American church of the ability to discern what has real, lasting eternal value and is inwardly transforming. It replaces discipleship with materialism and substitutes authentic Christianity for worldly religiosity.

There are many stories and Bible verses prosperity preachers like to use that are almost always pulled out of context. These false teachers have a knack for taking biblical truth and twisting it or repackaging it in a way that puts the focus on us rather than on God, much like Satan did to Eve in the garden of Eden.

Many like to use the promises to Abraham in the Old Testament as a basis for claiming materialistic entitlements today.[3] Others like to take the principle of sacrificial giving and redirect its motives from selflessness to reciprocating rewards and returns of monetary abundance.

Along this latter path of "giving in order to get," some false teachers have stolen the phrase *sowing one's seed* and the story that goes with it that Jesus used in one of his parables. Jesus often used parables as illustrations that helped teach about spiritual matters pertaining to the kingdom of God. Some stories were easy to understand and relate to, others more difficult.

But the story known as the parable of the sower or the parable of the soils is relatively easy to understand, primarily because Jesus himself interpreted the parable for his disciples in private. We then have the luxury of understanding what it truly means. Yet in spite of this, many false teachers find a way to give it new meaning in order to serve their own subversive purposes.

The story is found in all three of the Synoptic Gospels (Matthew, Mark, and Luke), but for our purposes we will focus on the account given to us by Mark, early in his gospel narrative. At this point in his ministry, Jesus had been known to have large crowds follow him due to the miracles he performed and the authority of his teaching. Within such large crowds there was bound to be a large variety of people—some hungry for truth, others looking for a miracle, some just curious, and others skeptical. It was a brilliant time for Jesus to teach about four kinds of hearts that the Word of God may encounter when it is preached—the hardened heart, the shallow heart, the carnal heart, and the receptive heart.

To be able to see and speak to the crowds clearly, Jesus gets into a boat and is in the bay while the people stay on the shoreline. He shares this parable:

> "Listen! Consider the sower who went out to sow. As he sowed, this occurred: Some seed fell along the path, and the birds came and ate it up. Other seed fell on rocky ground where it didn't have much soil, and it sprang up right away, since it didn't have deep soil. When the sun came up, it was scorched, and since it didn't have a root, it withered. Other seed fell among thorns, and the thorns came up and choked it, and it didn't produce a crop. Still others fell on good ground and produced a crop that increased 30, 60, and 100 times what was sown." Then He said, "Anyone who has ears to hear should listen!"
>
> Mark 4:3–9

The reality here is that Jesus is not talking about money. He's using an agricultural illustration to show the different kinds of reception the Word of God receives when it is proclaimed in a mixed company of people.

The seed that fell on the path and was immediately eaten without any crop represents the *hardened heart*. The seed that fell on the rocky soil that doesn't allow the seeds to take deep roots is the *shallow heart*. The seed that fell among the thorns that choked out, cut off, or stole the nutrients away from the seed represents the *carnal* or *worldly heart*. In each type of heart there is a lack of true saving faith in response to the seed sown (the Word of God).

But the good soil or good ground represents the *receptive, believing heart*. This is the soil that receives the seed and allows it to take root and produce fruit. It describes the heart of the true believer in Christ. There is real repentance and real belief, and the fruit that springs from it gives evidence of a changed life. This person has embraced the truth, it has taken root in their life, and they are growing spiritually and producing fruit for the glory of God.

Jesus' explanation helps us see what is happening spiritually.

> "The sower sows the word. These are the ones along the path where the word is sown: when they hear, immediately Satan comes and takes away the word sown in them. And these are the ones sown on rocky ground: when they hear the word, immediately they receive it with joy. But they have no root in themselves; they are short-lived. When pressure or persecution comes because of the word, they immediately stumble. Others are sown among thorns; these are the ones who hear the word, but the worries of this age, the seduction of wealth, and the desires for other things enter in and choke the word, and it becomes unfruitful. But the ones sown on good ground are those who hear the word, welcome it, and produce a crop: 30, 60, and 100 times what was sown."
>
> Mark 4:14–20

This parable is about the Word of God being "sown as seed" in the world where there is a spiritual battle taking place, where some hearts are hardened toward the things of God, some are distracted and experience-oriented without much depth, some are sucked into and seduced by the trappings of the world that is sold out to self-gratification and the lusts of the flesh, and others are hungry, thirsty, and open toward the truth of God found in the gospel.

Here is where the prosperity preacher twists the meaning of the parable for his or her own benefit. Many of them will say that Jesus teaches the *principle* of sowing seeds of faith with the promise of a monetary return. It's true that the parable teaches that real faith will produce fruit, but it is quite a stretch to take a parable about the heart's receptiveness to the Word of God and use it as a mechanism for weaseling people out of money.

The parable is not about giving money at all. It is not about sowing the seed of faith in any monetary sense in order to get a return. Rather, it is about preaching the Word of God in mixed company, knowing the true believer who receives it by faith will walk away with a life that will bear fruit. The Word of God will bring forth a harvest of righteousness among those who truly receive it by faith.

Recently I watched a video of a false teacher asking his listeners to sow a seed of $54.17 to his ministry in order to "focus your faith" and to take a stand opposing "every devil loosed against you, your family, and your future." He called it an "Isaiah 54:17 no-weapon seed." The prophecy of Isaiah 54:17 says,

> No weapon that is formed against you will prosper; and
> every tongue that accuses you in judgment you will condemn.

This is the heritage of the servants of the LORD, and their vindication is from Me, declares the LORD.

NASB

Yet this passage in Isaiah is a prophetic promise of God's protection of his people that will be ultimately fulfilled when Jesus comes to earth a second time to reign over his people, whereby he will shield and protect them from all enemies. But this false teacher has taken the passage out of context, repackaged it along with the seed-sowing principle, and is promising an "active miracle of protection against the devil," right here, right now against Satan's weapons of "disease, divorce, discouragement, doubt, or death." Somehow, sowing the seed of $54.17 will help you declare victory and prosper by activating your faith in such a way that opposes "the devils loosed against you."

This kind of sick, twisted manipulation of Scripture in order to conjure up money for a man's ministry is the type of deception prosperity preachers thrive on. To be fair, believers are to go to battle by putting on the armor of God described in Ephesians 6:10–18, none of which prescribes the giving of money to a ministry as a means of focusing your faith so that you can take a greater stand and declare victory.

As a general rule, Christians should be very cautious whenever they hear a pastor or televangelist using the parable of the soils or the sower as a means of invoking the need to give to a ministry for the purpose of activating their faith and taking a stand against the devil. It's not what that story is about.

The preacher will tell you that by sending in the funds, you are keeping the devil from prospering against you, but in reality that money is going to help prosper the preacher, who himself is teaching the doctrine of demons (1 Timothy 4:1). So in the end, it prospers the devil after all, since it helps prop up a ministry that is all about deception and greed.

This misuse of a biblical story of seed sowing reminds us of the principle of reading Scripture in context with specific attention to the main point of the story, which thankfully Jesus makes abundantly clear without much need for guessing.

Beware of those who extract biblical phrases and reapply them to foreign contexts in a way that undermines the useful truth that comes from that original phrase. Satan is a master at taking truth and twisting it ever so slightly, but in this case the twist is more than just a slight turn; it is rather a severing of its meaning altogether with the motive of preying on the weak and vulnerable.

The prosperity gospel promises what it cannot deliver and it sells something that you should not buy. Paul said to the Galatians that if anyone preaches a gospel other than the true gospel of Jesus Christ, let there be a curse on that one (Galatians 1:8–9). Jude, the Lord's half brother, warned us about false teachers:

> For some men, who were designated for this judgment long ago, have come in by stealth; they are ungodly, turning the grace of our God into promiscuity and denying Jesus Christ, our only Master and Lord. . . . These are the ones who are like dangerous reefs at your love feasts. They feast with you, nurturing only themselves without fear. They are waterless clouds carried along by winds; trees in late autumn—fruitless, twice dead, pulled out by the roots; wild waves of the sea,

foaming up their shameful deeds; wandering stars for whom the blackness of darkness is reserved forever!

Jude 4, 12–13

Let us not be naïve. Let us put on the full armor of God against this kind of false gospel and against these kinds of false teachers, so that their weapons of warfare may not prosper against us.

9

The "Three" Wise Men

"For we saw his star when it rose and have come to worship him."

—Matthew 2:2 ESV

It is a common question that comes to those in church leadership, a question that sounds like this: "Where does the Bible talk about [insert topic here]?" These inquiries come often and are a good reminder of why it's important for all Christians to be committed to studying the Bible for themselves.[1]

As you can probably imagine, pastors field a wide range of Bible-related questions. Some are easy to answer, and some are more difficult. The Bible directly addresses many topics, but not all. And it's also not uncommon to be asked about ideas and concepts that are not actually in the Bible, such as the popular but erroneous idea that God helps those who help themselves. It is precisely because we can't help ourselves that God sent his Son Jesus to save us from our sin.

Further, many ideas that people think are in the Bible stem from *church tradition* rather than Scripture. The concept of purgatory is one of those. The idea that there is a place where the souls of the departed go to be purified before they are eligible for heaven is nowhere found in Scripture and is theologically problematic, as it would be an affront to the sufficient sacrifice of Christ on the cross to fully atone for our sins.[2]

Still others confuse *sacred holiday tradition* for Scripture. One of the more famous misuses of tradition that is often *read back into* Scripture comes from a familiar Christmas carol written by John Henry Hopkins Jr. in 1857, which we know today as "We Three Kings." At the time of its composition, Hopkins served as the rector of Christ Episcopal Church in Williamsport, Pennsylvania.

It is said that Hopkins wrote the piece for a Christmas pageant, although it wasn't formally published until 1863. Its original title is "Three Kings of Orient," and it is found in his work entitled *Carols, Hymns, and Songs*. It is a delightful piece to sing with a catchy tune that has found its way into children's programs at churches and schools across the country for decades.

It has become a part of sacred American Christian tradition to recount the story of the wise men from the East who came to offer gifts of gold, frankincense, and myrrh to the Christ child as an act of worship.

But a closer look into the account as recorded by Matthew will reveal many differences between the actual history of the event and the carol that we know and love. Now, to be fair, no one likes people who take something fun and spoil it for everyone by attempting to be technical about everything. Indeed, that is not my intent.

The reason why I have included this chapter is because I believe we need to understand what Scripture teaches when it comes to the various practices and traditions of the church, the songs that we sing, and what it is that shapes our view of the story of Christ.

First, it will be good to take a close look at the story itself and its particulars. We begin with Matthew's account in chapter 2.

> After Jesus was born in Bethlehem of Judea in the days of King Herod, wise men from the east arrived unexpectedly in Jerusalem, saying, "Where is He who has been born King of the Jews? For we saw His star in the east and have come to worship Him."
>
> vv. 1–2

King Herod the Great was the first of a long line of Herods who ruled the Holy Land during the reign of the Roman Empire. He ruled from 37 BC to 4 BC, which would have put the birth of Christ somewhere around 5 BC. He was a rather ruthless and brutal man, who was quick to put down any rivals to his throne, whether actual or potential.[3]

Herod was powerful and wealthy, very cunning and clever, and administratively gifted. He is responsible for some of the greatest architectural feats and building projects in Israel, including the palace-fortress at Masada, and perhaps most significantly, the Temple Mount in Jerusalem. Herod taxed the people heavily, likely to help fund his projects.

He was a tyrant who loved power and was rather paranoid. "In his last years," writes New Testament scholar D. A. Carson, "suffering an illness that compounded his paranoia, he turned to cruelty and in fits of rage and jealousy killed close associates, his wife Mariamne . . . and at least two of his sons."[4]

So when the wise men from the East came to him asking about a king, you can see why Herod's paranoia would cause him great concern (which in the end would lead him to slaughter all males in Bethlehem, age two and under, after the visit and eventual trek back home of the wise men).

The first common mistake people make about the story is that the wise men (or *magi* in the original Greek) were not kings. They were likely magicians, philosophers, priests, and astrologers from Persia (modern-day Iran). They were highly esteemed and educated, and at times were known to practice medicine even as a physician would.

Further, even though they were Gentiles, they were likely familiar with Jewish prophecy concerning a coming king, since many Jews were still scattered in their region because of the exile (of the Old Testament) and the current Roman occupation.[5]

Second, their mode of transportation is not mentioned—it could have been camels or chariots, or they could have walked. This aspect of the story is not that significant, and it is not inappropriate to imagine them or portray them on camels since this is a valid mode of transportation in that region even today.

Being familiar with astrology, the wise men would have seen the "star in the east" as an anomaly, and likely searched the Jewish Scriptures for some indication of what it might mean. The word used for "star" by Matthew could mean any bright radiance or celestial light in the sky, and some have suggested this was either a comet, a supernova of some type, an alignment of planets, or better yet a supernatural manifestation of the Shekinah, the glory of God (which led the Israelites through the desert under Moses in the Old Testament. See Exodus 13:21).

Moved by the "star," the wise men see it as a fulfilment of Jewish prophecy about a coming king, and they have come to pay homage and worship him. This obviously gripped the heart of King Herod with excitement, rage, and paranoia.

> When King Herod heard this, he was deeply disturbed, and all Jerusalem with him. So he assembled all the chief priests and scribes of the people and asked them where the Messiah would be born. "In Bethlehem of Judea," they told him, "because this is what was written by the prophet: And you, Bethlehem, in the land of Judah, are by no means least among the leaders of Judah: because out of you will come a leader who will shepherd My people Israel."
>
> Matthew 2:3–6

Not only was Herod disturbed, but the text says "and all Jerusalem with him." The people of Jerusalem knew Herod's temperament well, and they knew that if he thought a rival king was somewhere in his governing region, there would soon be bloodshed, perhaps several deaths. The public's anxiety increased dramatically whenever Herod's blood pressure mounted, and they feared his reaction to this news.

Hearing the story about the newborn king from the wise men, Herod decides to consult the experts, the Jewish chief priests and scribes who knew the prophecies well. They tell him the location of where the future ruler and Messiah is to be born, in Bethlehem. Interestingly, these chief priests and scribes do not follow up on all this even after they hear about it. They are seemingly indifferent. Herod is hostile, the chief priests and scribes are indifferent, and the wise men are interested in worship. I think it's fair to say that those three different reactions sum up most people's reactions to Jesus even today—hostility, indifference and apathy, or genuine worship.

Herod's investigation continues,

> Then Herod secretly summoned the wise men and asked them the exact time the star appeared. He sent them to Bethlehem and said, "Go and search carefully for the child. When you find Him, report back to me so that I too can go and worship Him."
>
> Matthew 2:7–8

It doesn't take a detective to figure out that Herod is up to something. Interestingly, in an attempt to find out how old this perceived threat of a king might actually be, Herod asks about the exact time the star appeared. As mentioned earlier, later in the story (Matthew 2:16–18), Herod will have all male children two and under killed in order to systematically do away with any "newborn king" threat from Bethlehem.

Herod commands the wise men to search for and find the child and to report back their findings, so that allegedly, he too "can go and worship Him." This lie had evil intentions behind it. Yet the wise men obey his command, at least at first.

> After hearing the king, they went on their way. And there it was—the star they had seen in the east! It led them until it

came and stopped above the place where the child was. When they saw the star, they were overjoyed beyond measure. Entering the house, they saw the child with Mary His mother, and falling to their knees, they worshiped Him. Then they opened their treasures and presented Him with gifts: gold, frankincense, and myrrh.

vv. 9–11

The wise men succeed in finding Jesus, thanks again to the "star" that reappeared in the sky directly above the place where Jesus was staying. And whereas Herod's heart is full of evil, the hearts of the wise men are "overjoyed beyond measure." They find Jesus and Mary (no mention of where Joseph is at this moment), and they fall down in worship.

Imagine the shock Mary must have had seeing these incredibly wealthy dignitaries from afar falling on their knees to worship her son. Even more amazing is what happens next—the presentation of the gifts.

We have gold, the precious metal of kings. We have frankincense, an incense that often served in priestly functions of worship services or anointings. And finally, we have myrrh, an expensive fragrance used by the rich, especially for burials. (Could it be that these gifts foreshadow the reality of Jesus as the King who was set apart to offer his own life unto death as the priestly sacrifice for our sins?)

All together, the gifts would have made Mary and Joseph (and Jesus) instantly wealthy, and may have helped fund their upcoming and rather sudden trip to Egypt to escape the rage of King Herod, who was bent on destroying the child. Thankfully, Joseph was warned by an angel in a dream about

Herod's plan, and thus they escaped Herod's (and ultimately Satan's) plan to eliminate the messianic threat.

Here is where we discover even more details that contradict our human traditions. It is assumed that *three* wise men made the journey to see Jesus simply because three different gifts were presented. But this is a false assumption. A caravan of such significance with the amount of wealth and materials accompanying them would likely have had more than three individuals in it. In fact, it's possible that the number of wise men could have been anywhere from five to ten or more. So there is no evidence that there are only three men, and it is not likely that they were kings.

What's more, the timing of their arrival may be anywhere from several months to a year or more after Jesus was born, and therefore this would preclude them from being at the actual site of the manger as recorded by the other gospel writer Luke, which is what most of us imagine in our nativity scenes.

How do we know this? There are at least two reasons. If you look closely at the text, it says in verse 11 that the wise men entered the house where they were staying. In the nativity story told by Luke, Jesus is not in a house. He's not even in the inn, but rather Mary is forced to give birth to him somewhere outside or in a cave near the animals (thus the manger, a feeding trough for the animals). So some time must have elapsed and some people must have left the busy region of Bethlehem before Joseph and Mary were able to get themselves into a house.[6]

Second, we know that by the time the wise men arrived to greet Jesus, it was at least forty or more days *after* his birth. This is due to the fact that in the gospel of Luke, Jesus was presented in the temple to be dedicated after the days of Mary's purification were complete, which according to Mosaic law (Leviticus 12) would be forty days.

Included in the dedication of the child, the mother (and presumably the father with her) would have also presented an offering of a one-year-old lamb and a pigeon or a turtledove. But if, due to money constraints, the mother could not afford to present a lamb, then two turtledoves or two pigeons could be offered in its place (Leviticus 12) to meet the required offerings.

Luke tells us that Joseph and Mary brought an offering of two turtledoves or two young pigeons to the dedication of Jesus (Luke 2:24), which would mean that they opted for the lesser offering due to their inability to pay for a year-old lamb.

But if the wise men had come to see Jesus while he was still in the manger (immediately after his birth), then Joseph and Mary would have had ample means (by virtue of the gold, frankincense, and myrrh) to pay the required offering of the lamb some forty days after his birth. Therefore, we can safely conclude that these wise men were not at the original manger scene as our human traditions like to portray.

So in summary, we have wise men or magi (not kings), and we have no evidence that there were only three of them or that they rode on camels. We cannot place these men at the manger scene, but rather they arrive much later to a house, and it is at least a couple of months or up to a year or more before they meet Jesus. So if we were to be historically and biblically accurate, the traditional manger scene would need some modification.

Will I still sing "We Three Kings" even though it is not technically correct? Of course. There is no reason to become legalistic about it, as if *not* singing it makes us any more spiritual than those who do sing it. But I will, in the back of my mind, remember that not all of our Christmas traditions are in complete alignment with the biblical story.

As the story concludes, we note how God intervenes supernaturally to preserve the life of the Christ child from the rage and fury of King Herod: "And being warned in a dream not to go back to Herod, they returned to their own country by another route" (Matthew 2:12).

God knew of Herod's plan, and in order to preserve the *divine plan*, he warned the wise men not to go back to Herod to tell him where the child was, which is what Herod requested. This is where many preachers of the Word see practical applications and parallels to the Christian life.

The wise men sought after and encountered Christ, worshiped him, gave of themselves sacrificially, and then went home another way—and in a spiritual sense, that's what happens with us. When we encounter Christ and are changed by him, we worship him and offer our lives as an offering to him, and then in the end, there's another way home for us. We may give him our time and treasures here on earth, but he has treasures waiting for us in heaven.

That will be our new home, and so just like the wise men, we are to encounter and worship him, avoid evil, and walk in a new way. There is so much to this simple story when we seek to understand it in context. Surely the main point of it is to show us God's divine plan—the sovereignty of God over evil and the inclusivity of the gospel by virtue of Gentiles who worship the rightful Jewish King—not just any king, but the King of kings. But there are other spiritual lessons as well.

So when it comes to our faith, *we should measure all our traditions* to the literal teaching of the Bible, understood properly in context. We should still sing and worship him in songs, in hymns, and in carols. But let us study the Word carefully so that we can sing joyfully about the truth—the truth about God and the truth about us. And like the wise men, we should offer worship, seek to avoid evil, and walk in a new way home.

10

The Betrayal of a Disciple: Judas

"Didn't I choose you, the Twelve? Yet one of you
is the Devil!"

—John 6:70

Judas Iscariot is a name that will live in infamy. And ever
since he betrayed Christ, difficult questions have arisen.
Was he truly a disciple? Was he saved? This chapter is going
to deal with these and other questions. But first, let's consider
some basic truths about Christianity, starting with eternal life.

Solomon himself said God has put eternity in our hearts
(Ecclesiastes 3:11), but it is hard for our finite minds to truly
fathom the reality of eternity—something that lasts not for
a time, or a season, but forever.

Jesus said, "Before Abraham was, I am" (John 8:58). This
is a statement of his eternal nature as God—that he has

existed even before the incarnation and even before Abraham was born. Moreover, it is a statement of his eternal existence. And he is the only one in the universe who can make that claim.

That said, since the moment we were conceived, we became eternal beings. Our souls will live eternally. The only question is, will we experience eternal life with God or eternal separation from the presence of God's blessing known as eternal death, or hell? Both are eternal places, but with a qualitatively different experience.

Undoubtedly, the book of the Bible that speaks the most about eternal life is the gospel of John. Jesus, on more than one occasion, made many promises about the nature of eternal life and the gift that is for everyone who believes in him. Perhaps one of my favorite quotes from Jesus is: "I assure you: Anyone who hears My word and believes Him who sent Me has eternal life and will not come under judgment but has passed from death to life" (John 5:24).

Here Jesus says that not only do we receive the promise of eternal life, we actually move from a state of spiritual death to spiritual life. And further, in the next verse he expands that life to the promise of a future *resurrected life* as well. So both spiritually and one day physically, all who believe in him will have life, and not just any life, but eternal life in the fullest sense! Jesus will see to this personally: "For this is the will of My Father: that everyone who sees the Son and believes in Him may have eternal life, and I will raise him up on the last day" (John 6:40).

Amazing! Something supernatural happens to believers when they genuinely repent of their sins and place their faith and trust in Jesus to save them from their sins. Paul, in one of his speeches in the book of Acts, states that Christ sent him to the Gentiles to preach the gospel in order "to open their eyes so they may turn from darkness to light and from the power of Satan to God, that by faith in Me they may receive forgiveness of sins and a share among those who are sanctified" (Acts 26:18).

Many spiritual realities are explained in this passage. The gospel has power to open our eyes, and saving faith will bring believers from *darkness* to *light*, from the power of *Satan* to *God*, as well as *forgiveness of sins* and an *inheritance* from God. These are no small truths. In fact, they are some of the most profound promises ever given to the believer in Christ.

Paul elsewhere explained that Christ "has rescued us from the domain of darkness and transferred us into the kingdom of the Son He loves" (Colossians 1:13).

Putting these ideas together, we are transferred from the realm of darkness to light and from the domain of darkness into the kingdom of the Son of God. We are now citizens of heaven (Philippians 3:20), sealed by the Spirit (Ephesians 1:13), and adopted children of God (Ephesians 1:5), who receive every spiritual blessing in Christ (Ephesians 1:3). The list of identity-shaping blessings and undeniably rich promises given to the true believer is monumental.

Jesus provided assurance that those who are his sheep will hear his voice and follow him. They will be given the promise of eternal life and will never perish, and no one will be able to "snatch them out of My hand" (John 10:28).

So the evidence is overwhelming that those who are truly born again cannot be "unborn again," and those who are given the Spirit are sealed by the Spirit and have the assurance that "he who began a good work in you will bring it to completion at the day of Jesus Christ" (Philippians 1:6 ESV).

Our salvation is a gift of God, who has promised that it will be eternal in nature, never to be lost or taken away. Therefore, we can have assurance that our salvation is secure. It is a gift that will never be revoked or taken back, and Jesus has placed his reputation on it and made it clear that the Spirit's job is to bring it to completion.

But what about people who at one time or another have professed to believe in Christ, who may have even seemed to display overwhelming evidence of spiritual fruit, but for some reason or another have completely abandoned Christ, rejected the faith, and walked away in seeming unbelief?

How could this happen if they were truly saved? Have they somehow lost their salvation? Is it possible they have been snatched out of Jesus' hand, so to speak? If so, what does this say about Jesus' promise?

This is undoubtedly a very serious and difficult issue to consider, especially when the person who has seemingly walked away from the faith is a family member, perhaps a son or a daughter, or even someone you respected who at one time served as your pastor or spiritual leader. Yes, there are times when life can deal us shockingly unexpected and unforeseen blows.

The apostle John knew the heartrending realities of this when there were people in the early church who were at one time professing Christ and walking in the way of discipleship, but eventually abandoned the faith, walked away from the church, and embraced false teachings. And some of them were teachers in the church! The conclusion he wanted the church to come to was this:

They went out from us, but they were not of us; for if they had been of us, they would have continued with us. But they went out, that it might become plain that they all are not of us.

1 John 2:19 ESV

John essentially says a true believer will persevere and remain in the faith, but if this does not happen, we may conclude that they never were genuinely saved to begin with. As hard as this may seem, it happens, and perhaps the definitive example of this is found in the Gospels with the story of the man they eventually called the Betrayer, Judas Iscariot.

Judas was one of the chosen twelve that Jesus had personally called to be by his side. Because of this, many assume that in order to be such a close follower of Jesus, Judas must have been a true believer with saving faith. He was a part of the group in Matthew 10 that was sent out to preach the gospel and who was also given authority over evil spirits, sickness, and disease (vv. 1–4).[1]

Does this mean, then, as some have erroneously suggested, that a true follower of Christ could actually receive salvation and then lose it by choosing to walk away? As we know, Judas eventually walked away and betrayed Jesus, selling him into the hands of the chief priests and officers for thirty pieces of silver (the price of a slave). There could be no worse abandonment than that.

I remember, as a child growing up, that there was a leader in my home church who suggested to me the story of Judas Iscariot was definitive evidence that someone could lose their salvation. As a kid, the thought of this horrified me and made me feel insecure about the whole thing.

I remember thinking, *Could this happen to me? Could I be saved one moment and then sin in another and lose my salvation? How would I know if I lost it? Would I feel God leave me? And if so, would I have to accept Christ all over again, and how many times would I have to do this, since I tend to sin every day?*

These might seem like silly questions, but I assure you this was where my brain went. It got so bad, I used to think that if I was ever in a car accident, somehow right before impact I would ask Jesus into my heart once again just in case I didn't survive. That way I would have a clean slate right before my heart stopped and know I was saved. What a low and diminished view of God's grace that was.

Let me assure you, this line of thinking is not from God, and is not biblical for all the reasons discussed earlier in this chapter. What then do we do with the story of Judas? How do we categorize this "disciple," who at one time followed Jesus, but eventually betrayed him and later took his own life?

First, let me make this clear, *Judas was not a true believer in Christ.* Even though he was chosen to be a part of Jesus' original twelve, this did not guarantee he was a man of saving faith in Christ. Many who followed Christ at one time walked away. In John 6, Jesus said some rather difficult things, including,

> Anyone who eats My flesh and drinks My blood has eternal life, and I will raise him up on the last day, because My flesh is real food and My blood is real drink. The one who eats My flesh and drinks My blood lives in Me, and I in him.
>
> vv. 54–56

Jesus was not speaking literally here, but rather figuratively and metaphorically about his impending death on the cross. It was this sacrificial death on the cross that the Jews would have to accept in order to receive the gift of eternal life. But for them, this was too difficult to understand and certainly too difficult to accept, since many of them had a militaristic and political image of what a Messiah should be.

Notice what happened next. John says, "From that moment many of His disciples turned back and no longer accompanied Him" (John 6:66).

Many walked away. And Jesus knew many were offended and that there were many of them who did not truly believe. What is astounding is what Jesus said to the rest of his followers:

> Jesus, knowing in Himself that His disciples were complaining about this, asked them, "Does this offend you? . . . The Spirit is the One who gives life. The flesh doesn't help at all. The words that I have spoken to you are spirit and are life. But there are some among you who don't believe." (For Jesus knew from the beginning those who would not believe and the one who would betray Him.)
>
> vv. 61–64

If this were not enough evidence to convince us, then maybe what Jesus said next will. He asked the twelve whether they wanted to go away too, and Peter spoke up: "Lord, who will we go to? You have the words of eternal life. We have come to believe and know that You are the Holy One of God!" (John 6:68–69).

Of course, Peter included all twelve disciples in that statement, but what he didn't know was what Jesus was now going to make clear. Jesus responded to Peter's statement by making an earth-shattering statement of his own: "'Didn't I choose you, the Twelve? Yet one of you is the Devil!'" Then the gospel writer John explained, "He was referring to Judas, Simon Iscariot's son, one of the Twelve, because he was going to betray Him" (John 6:70–71).

Some translations have Jesus saying, "One of you is *a* devil." Either way, whether Jesus called Judas a devil, or figuratively speaking called him the Devil himself is beside the point. The point is, this Judas was not a true follower of Jesus—he was completely lost, taken captive by Satan, and was destined to betray Jesus.

Now, some may say, "Wait a minute! Didn't Jesus turn to Peter at one point and say, 'Get behind Me, Satan!' and essentially call the future leader of the church 'the devil' as well (Mark 8:31–33)? How then is Peter not lost just as Judas was?"

The difference is that Jesus was rebuking Peter, who was vehemently rebuking Jesus for any idea that he was going to Jerusalem to die on some cross. Peter never wanted to let his beloved Messiah suffer such a fate. And what Jesus heard was "Satan's agenda" behind such an ignorant statement.

That's why Jesus said, "Get behind Me, Satan," to let Peter know his understanding was so far off from God's will that it was not God's concerns he was thinking about, but man's, and ultimately Satan's agenda.

But there is a difference in Peter's ignorantly asserting man's agenda (which would coincide with Satan's plans to usurp God's will) versus actually being called a devil, who would completely walk away and betray him for good like Judas did. The former is a foolish and ignorant momentary mistake; the latter is a purposeful and willful rejection of

Jesus *that will go all the way to the end in death*. Peter made mistakes, but he loved Jesus, and the rest of his life proved that beyond a doubt. The same cannot be said for Judas.

So Jesus called Judas a devil, and John called him a betrayer, essentially a tool of Satan. That hardly sounds like a commendation for a true believer. But further evidence of Judas's spiritual state is seen in the last moments with Jesus' disciples before his crucifixion while he was eating with them at the Last Supper. In John 13, Jesus once again announces his betrayer while eating the Passover with his disciples, and once again it is Judas.

Further, in the course of the chapter, we see Judas as the one who was deemed "unclean" by Jesus, meaning not spiritually washed (13:11). Additionally, it was Judas who was said to be possessed by Satan (13:27) as he left to betray Jesus, as he was destined to do. And clearly it was Judas that Jesus was referring to when he was praying to the Father and talked about the "son of destruction," the one follower of his twelve who was "lost" (17:12).

None of these terms could be used of a true believer and follower of Christ. Believers are not destined for destruction and are not lost—in fact, we are the "found ones" who have been rescued by our Savior.

Judas was a thief who was full of greed and jealousy (John 12:4–6), causing Jesus to say, "Woe to that man by whom He is betrayed" (Luke 22:22). His guilt did not lead him to true repentance and faith but to suicide (Matthew 27:5).[2] He gives no evidence of believing and trusting in Jesus as the Messiah who would save him.

Judas does not give us enough evidence to suggest that he was ever a true believer in Jesus Christ. In fact, the way Jesus talks about him and the narrative description of his actions and character suggest the very opposite. Therefore, the story of Judas could never be used as evidence that a true believer could lose their salvation. The very idea of losing something that God designed to be eternal is a contradiction.

The preponderance of evidence throughout Scripture is that a true believer's salvation is secure. Though God is the only one who truly knows the heart, we are told to be fruit inspectors, taking stock of even our own lives to see whether we are walking in the faith.

We need not worry or be concerned that the gift we were given and the new life we have been promised will ever be lost or taken away. God is faithful to his promises. His character and reputation depend on it. Indeed, he who began a good work in you will carry it on to completion (Philippians 1:6).

So this story is a sad one, but it's not a believer's story. It is the sad story of a man who walked with Jesus but never truly believed, and I am saddened that many people who sit in church are on the same path. May we truly preach the gospel of God's grace and preach repentance and faith, so that those who hear and follow the Shepherd's voice can rest assured that they have crossed over from death to life, from darkness to light, and are eternally secure.

11

The Samaritan Pentecost

For we were all baptized by one Spirit into one body.

—1 Corinthians 12:13

One of the more popular methods Satan uses to confuse Christians involves doublespeak or double-talk. This is the idea that someone may use Christian *terms*, but the terms do not possess traditional Christian *meanings*. For example, people from the Mormon faith call themselves *Christians* even though they do not believe the historic doctrines and teachings of the Christian faith.[1]

Further, Mormons may say they believe Jesus is the Son of God, but what they mean is that he is a son of *a* god and his goddess wife who gave birth to his spirit and his "spirit brother" Lucifer in heaven before Jesus took on human existence here on earth. In this sense, there are many "sons of the gods" and Jesus is just one of them. In fact, Mormonism teaches that all men have the potential to become gods in the afterlife, and along with their wives will be able to produce spirit children and repopulate their own planet.[2]

So when it comes to evangelizing and sharing your faith with a Mormon (or even a Jehovah's Witness), it is important that within the conversation there is an attempt to define the terms that are being used, otherwise assumptions are made when in fact we may be talking past each other and using terms and ideas much differently.

This is an important concept to grasp when it comes to sharing the gospel with people who are known to be outside the traditional understanding of the Christian faith. But confusing terms, phrases, and ideas are common within the confines of the traditional orthodox Christian church as well. For example, if someone tells you God has a plan to give you an *abundant life*, it is important that you seek to clarify what they mean by "abundant." For in John 10:10, Jesus was talking about the abundant *spiritual life* right here and now, not some Americanized health and wealth idea whereby he wants you to always be in good health and financially well off as long as you have enough faith.

The same is true for the word *good* in Romans 8:28. If God is working all things together for good, we need to be careful that we don't import our own definition of *good* into that verse and hold God hostage to act accordingly. God's definition of *good* is seen in the very next verse (v. 29), whereby the greatest good that God is working us toward is to be more like his Son in character and holiness, and he is weaving together the good and the bad we face to accomplish this goal.[3]

This brings us to a story and a phrase in the book of Acts that has left many Christians confused. We'll get to the story in a minute, but the phrase is the *baptism of the Holy Spirit*, and it is more common in certain Pentecostal or charismatic circles, although all Christians in any denomination should be familiar with it, for it is an important biblical phrase that has a life-changing meaning to it.

Let's understand a little about the origins of this phrase. There are seven passages in the New Testament where the phrase *baptism in/with/by the Holy Spirit* is used. John the Baptist first used it to describe Jesus' ministry in distinction from his own. "I have baptized you with water, but He will baptize you *with the Holy Spirit*" (Mark 1:8).

> I baptize you with water for repentance, but the One who is coming after me is more powerful than I. I am not worthy to remove His sandals. He Himself will baptize you with the Holy Spirit and fire.
>
> Matthew 3:11[4]

> John answered them all, "I baptize you with water, but One is coming who is more powerful than I. I am not worthy to untie the strap of His sandals. He will baptize you *with the Holy Spirit* and fire."
>
> Luke 3:16[5]

> I didn't know Him, but He who sent me to baptize with water told me, "The One you see the Spirit descending and resting on—He is the One who *baptizes with the Holy Spirit*."
>
> John 1:33

John introduces this phrase in the New Testament, and whatever it may mean to be baptized by/in/with the Holy Spirit (the Greek word is *baptizō*, meaning "to immerse"), it is something that is ascribed to Jesus whereby he will do it to his followers.[6]

However, as theologian Wayne Grudem points out, the phrase *baptism of* or *baptized with the Holy Spirit* is used later to directly refer to *Pentecost* in Acts 1:5 and Acts 11:16. It is here we see the Holy Spirit given in fullness to the church, whereby he dwelt permanently, for the first time, in the hearts of all who believed in and received Jesus as Lord. At this Pentecost event, great power was given to the disciples, who were enabled to speak in foreign tongues, preach the Word, and witness to the gospel in keeping with what Jesus predicted would happen in Acts 1:8. Therefore, when the time Jesus predicted came to fruition, the disciples were immersed by/with/in the Holy Spirit and these unique gifts came with it.

However, this was a *unique transitional event* in the time-line of biblical history, and here is where the confusion starts.

Some Christians, erroneously, I would argue, have concluded that when a Christian today is baptized by the Holy Spirit, that very same Pentecost experience is repeated *in the exact same way* as before, mainly in that the experience will always manifest itself in speaking in tongues. This, however, ignores the unique transitional nature of Pentecost.

The Acts 2 Pentecost was a one-time event in the life of the church whereby the transition from the old covenant to the new covenant was taking place and the international nature of the gospel was first being revealed. At this never-seen-before moment when the Spirit was being given in fullness, God

117

supernaturally enabled them to speak in foreign tongues to fellow Jews who heard them in their own native language, a sign of God's affirmation and endorsement of the gospel message.

So the gift was special to that day. But there is no evidence that every Christian in the New Testament who came to faith in Jesus spoke in tongues as evidence of the Spirit's presence, even if it did happen to all or most of the believers gathered there on that day.

Instead, speaking in tongues was later seen as a unique spiritual gift in the church that was given to a select few individuals (see 1 Corinthians 12:10, 30). And no matter if one believes or does not believe that this gift is still operational in the church today as a sign and source of divine revelation, we cannot conclude that all believers experienced that gift even in the first century, and we cannot conclude that all believers must experience that gift today as evidence of the Holy Spirit in their lives.

So what *can* we conclude regarding the baptism of the Holy Spirit?

This is where the apostle Paul clears things up for us. Paul told the Corinthians that all believers then, and by implication all believers today, will experience this spiritual baptism if they have truly repented from sin and have placed their faith in Christ alone for their salvation. In other words, the immersion, or baptism by/with/in the Holy Spirit is paramount to the initial activity of the Holy Spirit in the life of a believer when he or she comes to faith for the first time and receives the indwelling Holy Spirit. For Paul said to the church in Corinth, "For we were all baptized by one Spirit into one body—whether Jews or Greeks, whether slaves or free—and we were all made to drink of one Spirit" (1 Corinthians 12:13).

Notice that Paul said, "We were *all baptized* by one Spirit" into one body (the church). Therefore, Paul is saying that *all Christians* received this baptism, and as a result they were immediately adopted and spiritually brought into the church, the one body of Christ.

The timing of this is important. Believers are brought into God's kingdom and are included in the church at the moment they believe and are saved. Therefore, this baptism and inclusion in the church is not something that happens later, after conversion, but is something that happens at the very moment of conversion, saving faith, or belief, and all believers receive it. At the moment of salvation, we are baptized with the Holy Spirit.

As Grudem remarks, "In this way 'baptism in the Holy Spirit' refers to all that the Holy Spirit does at the beginning of our Christian lives."[7] Yes, the disciples were true believers for a while before they received this baptism, but "they were living at the time of transition between the old covenant work of the Holy Spirit and the new covenant work of the Holy Spirit . . . [and therefore] it is not to be taken as a pattern for us, for we are not living at a time of transition in the work of the Holy Spirit."[8]

Now, if this is the case, why do some people in Pentecostal and charismatic circles refer to an additional baptism of the Holy Spirit that may happen long after their conversion, and why do they appeal to another passage in Acts (8:14–25) as biblical support for it?

There is much to say here. But before we draw any conclusions, let's take a look at this often misunderstood and misused story in Acts 8 and put it in its context. First, note that the phrase *baptism of the Holy Spirit* appears nowhere in this text. Second, this is another transitional moment, as the gospel is now for the first time being believed by a people group other than the Jews—the Samaritans. Let's look at the text closely.

> When the apostles who were at Jerusalem heard that Samaria had welcomed God's message, they sent Peter and John to them. After they went down there, they prayed for them, so the Samaritans might receive the Holy Spirit. For He had not yet come down on any of them; they had only been baptized in the name of the Lord Jesus. Then Peter and John laid their hands on them, and they received the Holy Spirit.
>
> vv. 14–17

For those who believe there can be a second baptism of the Holy Spirit subsequent to conversion, this text is often used to support that view. They may say that what you see here are true believers in Christ who did not receive the Holy Spirit until later, after their initial belief, and that this somehow legitimizes the idea that a subsequent baptism of the Spirit is indeed possible.

It is true that we certainly have believers who have received and believed the gospel. For earlier in verse 12, it is Philip the Evangelist who shares the gospel for the first time to a group of Samaritans who believe in it and who are then physically baptized in water as a testimony to their public belief and spiritual cleansing in keeping with the commands of Jesus (Matthew 28:19–20).

But once again, we have another major transition moment in the history of the New Testament gospel. Up to this point, the gospel had primarily been believed and received by Jewish believers, but now the gospel is being received and believed by a once-hated apostate people group that Jews would have never associated with—the Samaritans.

In the mind of a Jewish believer, they may have asked, "Could this be true? Is it possible that God is going to include *these* people in the church as well?" (and later, the Gentiles; see Acts 10:44–46). This would have been highly controversial to the point that the apostles themselves would need to verify and answer that question once and for all in person.

Therefore, it seems that God awaited the arrival of the apostles on the scene, in order to see for themselves before he chose to baptize these new Samaritan believers with the Holy Spirit. In this way, it was necessary for the apostles to verify this new major development, especially since it involved the bitter rivals of the Jewish people, the Samaritans.

From then on, whenever believers came to faith, they were immediately baptized by and permanently indwelt with the Holy Spirit in keeping with what Paul told the Corinthians (1 Corinthians 12:13), and there is no evidence that everyone was given the spiritual gift of tongues.

If we remember that the book of Acts is a transitional book, we will not make the mistake of thinking that everything that happened then should also be happening now. It is meant to be a description of that unique moment in history, as God's people transitioned from the old covenant to the new covenant. It was not meant to be a *prescription* for how the church was supposed to operate today. The Holy Spirit was being poured out on the church for the first time, but now that that transition is complete, we should not expect those initial transitional experiences to be repeated in the same way today.

We do not have apostles anymore, and we do not see people being raised from the dead or miraculously disappearing like we do in Acts. The book reflects a unique moment in history and is not meant to be a textbook for the pattern of the church today.

It is true that moments of great blessing can follow a believer's salvation. For example, we may experience more of the Spirit's control in our lives as we repent of sin and seek God's will for our lives. We may find ourselves uniquely impacted by a sermon or a book where the message has life-changing power to it. Maybe it is a Christian song that strikes a chord with our life and reaches into the depths of our souls and brings change.

Still others, as they study the Bible, experience God's presence in prayer or worship, or find renewed joy in fellowshipping with other believers, may see some measurable spiritual growth that comes through the power of the Spirit.

In all these experiences, the term *baptism of the Holy Spirit* is not the proper way to describe those things, because that term describes the initial pouring out of the Spirit at the beginning of the Christian life. Perhaps it would be better to say that subsequent experiences are times when we are filled afresh with the Holy Spirit in such a way that he has more control of us and we are more submissive to him, thus making his presence uniquely felt. Paul said,

> Pay careful attention, then, to how you walk—not as unwise people but as wise—making the most of the time, because

the days are evil. So don't be foolish, but understand what the Lord's will is. And don't get drunk with wine, which leads to reckless actions, but be filled by the Spirit: speaking to one another in psalms, hymns, and spiritual songs, singing and making music from your heart to the Lord, giving thanks always for everything to God the Father in the name of our Lord Jesus Christ, submitting to one another in the fear of Christ.

Ephesians 5:15–21

Being filled with the Spirit is a better way to understand and describe these times of great growth or renewal in our faith. When we first believe, we are baptized and indwelt with the Holy Spirit. We receive all of him. Yet it is also true that as we grow he fills our lives with spiritual growth as we submit to him.

This is a case where a biblical term is misused because its context has been misunderstood, and it has been misapplied to experiences today in a way that causes us to lose its original meaning. Therefore, careful study of words, terms, and ideas in context will help us make sense of it all. Further, knowing the background of a book also enlightens us, especially a transitional book like the book of Acts.

When I moved to Florida over a decade ago, I noticed right away that they called Coca-Cola and Pepsi-Cola and other like products *soda*. Where I come from, we called them *pop*, while people in other parts of the country call them *coke* no matter what brand it is. Imagine how confusing this must be for a non-English-speaking visitor who is trying to figure out our terms.

The same is true for the Bible, but the stakes are much higher. We would do well as Christians to learn the language of the Bible in its various contexts so that we can all communicate God's truth in a clear and accurate way. And it is better to be filled with the Spirit than with pop or soda, anyway.

12

The Rich Fool

"One's life does not consist in the abundance of
the things he possesses."

—Luke 12:15 NKJV

Y ou have heard it said that the eyes are a window to the
soul. Most of us can take one good look at our loved
ones, and from their eyes quickly discern how they
may be doing mentally or emotionally. This is especially true
for parents, who seemingly have a knack for knowing what's
happening in the hearts of their children simply through
their eyes.

But that's not all. Not only can the eyes give us away, so
can the tone of our voice. To this day, my mother has a knack
for knowing how I'm doing when she hears my voice on the
phone long before I've told her *anything* substantial. It's

as if mothers have this supernatural sense of what is going on in their children's souls. And it's not fair. We can't hide anything!

With this in mind, how much more does the Maker of our souls have the ability to read and know our hearts? The apostle Paul tells us God is the one who "examines" (1 Thessalonians 2:4) and "searches" (Romans 8:27) the heart. God himself, through the prophet Jeremiah, emphatically stated, "I, the Lord, search the heart and test the mind" (Jeremiah 17:10 ESV). Nothing can be hidden from God, as he knows the secrets of our hearts (Psalm 44:21).

When God came to earth in the form of Jesus Christ, this ability to know and read the hearts of all people was uniquely put on display. Even before he met Nathanael, Jesus knew the heart of this future disciple and said, "Behold, an Israelite indeed, in whom there is no deceit!" (John 1:47 ESV).

Further, Jesus knew the hearts of the scribes and Pharisees (Luke 5:21–22), as well as those who were seemingly trusting in him as a result of seeing the signs he performed. In fact, he knew the hearts of all he encountered (John 2:23–25; Matthew 9:4; Luke 9:47; 11:17). Even the disciples were quick to see this (John 16:30; 21:17).

When it comes to the cries, burdens, or even the sins of our hearts, Jesus is fully aware of each one of them, which can either be comforting or disconcerting. He knows what we need, and he knows where we fall short. Thankfully, he is abundantly gracious.

Even so, Jesus is unafraid to point out areas of people's lives where change is needed. In Bible times, whether it was the scribes and Pharisees, the rich young ruler, or the people in his hometown who rejected him, Jesus could see weaknesses and blind spots that humans don't always see.

All of this leads to the Bible story known as the parable of the rich fool, which Jesus told after a man asked him to help settle a family dispute over an inheritance. Jesus knew the *real reason* why the man approached him.

Our story is found only in the book of Luke, and one of the major themes of this particular gospel is Luke's emphasis on the danger of riches. The Bible never says it is a sin to be wealthy or abundantly successful in business. One look at Abraham, or even Job, in the Old Testament and we see two extremely wealthy men whose hearts both pleased the Lord as they walked in faith.[1] But the Bible does warn us about the inherent dangers of loving money more than the things of God. Paul warned Timothy, telling him that the "*love* of money is a root of *all kinds of evil*" (1 Timothy 6:10), and that by craving it many people have brought much grief to their lives.

The problem is not in owning money, it's allowing that money to own you, or in other words, to consume your soul. Both the poor and the rich alike can be guilty of lusting after money. Jesus, elsewhere in Luke, warned against being mastered by money:

> No servant can serve two masters, for either he will hate the one and love the other, or he will be devoted to the one and despise the other. You cannot serve God and money.
>
> 16:13 ESV

When Jesus was asked to intervene on an inheritance issue, he knew it was merely a smoke screen for the hidden motive of the man's heart: a lust for money. And the parable Jesus told in order to expose the real issue has the potential to be widely misunderstood.

Here's the context for our story: Jesus had been warning the crowds about the dangers of fake religion, hypocrisy, and even blasphemy, when a man interrupted his teaching.

> Someone from the crowd said to Him, "Teacher, tell my brother to divide the inheritance with me."
>
> "Friend," He said to him, "who appointed Me a judge or arbitrator over you?"
>
> Luke 12:13–14

Nothing in the immediate context suggests that Jesus is talking about money issues, so apparently the impatient man wanted to change the subject so they could talk about him. It was a blunt interruption. At first glance it might seem that Jesus was a little snarky toward the man, but this was not the case. Jesus was simply putting up a boundary around a bold demand, whereby he was able to recognize the true motive behind it.

It was a traditional role for rabbis of that day to settle disputes and civil matters, and seeing Jesus' popularity and inherent authority, the man addressed Jesus as Rabbi or Teacher. Indeed, Jesus was a teacher, but not the formal, legally ordained kind of rabbi that would come much later in Jewish tradition.

We are not told any more details about the dispute between these brothers, but it doesn't make much difference to Jesus. He didn't come to earth to settle these kinds of disputes, and he knew the man didn't really want arbitration, but rather wanted Jesus to "decide against his brother."[2] He saw completely through it, and decided to deal with the *motive* instead of the matter at hand: "He then told them, 'Watch out and be on guard against all greed because one's life is not in the abundance of his possessions'" (Luke 12:15).[3]

Mercy! Jesus doesn't mess around. He has a way about him, doesn't he? He immediately puts his finger on the *real* issue. The man's problem was greed, surfacing in a battle over an inheritance. He wasn't truly interested in justice; rather, he was lusting after "stuff." And Jesus knew it. He could see that the man's security and identity were wrapped up in the pursuit of wealth, the love of money.

To illustrate his warning in a poignant fashion, Jesus turned to what he did best, storytelling. So he pulled out a parable that told a story with a spiritual punch.

> Then He told them a parable: "A rich man's land was very productive. He thought to himself, 'What should I do, since I don't have anywhere to store my crops? I will do this,' he said. 'I'll tear down my barns and build bigger ones and store all my grain and my goods there. Then I'll say to myself, "You have many goods stored up for many years. Take it easy; eat, drink, and enjoy yourself."'
>
> "But God said to him, 'You fool! This very night your life is demanded of you. And the things you have prepared—whose will they be?'"
>
> Luke 12:16–20

Taking this story out of the aforementioned context could easily lead someone to draw different conclusions about what Jesus was actually saying. It has the potential to be misunderstood. Some may fear that Jesus is discouraging anyone from saving money or allowing themselves to enjoy the abundant fruit that comes from their labors. But to draw those conclusions would be a mistake.

First, as previously mentioned, there is nothing inherently wrong with being rich or even having land that produces an abundance of crops. In fact, this man was truly blessed. All the factors that need to come together for a farmer to have a bumper crop have fallen in place for this man.

But issues surface when blessings come, and this is always the case when someone is confronted with the "burden" of success. What's the man's next move? Either he could be thankful and share generously with others less fortunate, or he could decide to keep it all to himself, pad his pocket even more, and live a selfish life of indulgence.

Clearly, in this story, the rich man chose the second option. His inward thoughts brought him to the point where he was willing to spend money tearing down the old just so he could spend even more money building something bigger. And once that was accomplished, he planned to prop his feet up and throw himself a party. With blessing there is always responsibility, but this man embraced an arrogant, selfish, and completely irresponsible way of life.

He made a killing and then gorged himself on the spoils instead of expressing his gratitude to God by being generous to those around him. It is always a good idea to remember that the Lord gives and the Lord takes away (Job 1:21), and with that principle in mind, when we choose to give generously out of what God has given us, we can rest assured that God always has a bigger shovel and can generously resupply *as we continue to give generously and sacrificially in faith*. It all comes from him and ultimately belongs to him.

But this mentality was not a part of the lifestyle of this rich farmer. Rather, he was full of greed, and what he didn't realize is that his time on earth was up. "Just when the man imagined himself to be set for life, God took his life . . . he had foolishly forgotten God (cf. Psalm 14:1; 53:1), as well as his own mortality."[4]

Instead of storing up treasure in heaven (by thanking God and generously sharing some of this earthly treasure), the man decided to indulge in his treasure here and now. He traded the eternal for the temporal, which sadly, so many people in this life choose to do. And just when he thought his life was as good as it gets, his life was over. Gone. Finished.

Then what does he have to show for his life? A life of greed that will not be rewarded. As the old saying goes, "You can't take it with you." You've probably heard the joke that there aren't too many armored cars that follow hearses these days.

It reminds me of a modern-day story of a woman whose selfish and greedy husband passed away. Just before they sealed his coffin for burial, she took out their checkbook and wrote him a check for the entire amount in the account and placed it in the coffin with him. Good luck cashing that check!

As Jesus said, "You fool! This very night your life is demanded of you. And the things you have prepared—whose will they be?" (Luke 12:20). In the end, the goods of the greedy husband belonged to the scorned and overlooked wife. Justice was done.

In the rich farmer's story, we don't know who will enjoy the spoils, which makes it even more tragic. What a fool indeed.

Unfortunately, we don't see the rest of the story or find out what happens to the man who was demanding justice concerning an inheritance either, but Luke doesn't leave any doubt as to what Jesus wanted us to learn.

It is often the case that the main point of a parable comes at the very end, and Jesus makes his point abundantly clear here: "That's how it is with the one who stores up treasure for himself and is not rich toward God" (Luke 12:21).

Jesus makes it clear that the riches that matter are not material in nature, but spiritual. Paul asked, "What do you have that you didn't *receive*?" (1 Corinthians 4:7). In other words, all that we are and all that we have are dependent upon God above. The very breath and health we enjoy and the ability to use our gifts, talents, and skills to make money or to have any measure of success completely depend on the grace of God.

Therefore, what room is there for boasting or indulgence or self-congratulations when it comes to the ways we are blessed? Does it not all come from God? And will it not all stay behind here on earth long after we're gone?

The story of the rich fool gets to the heart of why we do the things we do and what it is we long for and why. Life, according to the book of James, is but a vapor, here one day and gone the next. The longer you live, the more you understand how fast life goes. And we have a choice to make: Are we going to live for the moment and the glory of self, or are we going to live for the glory of God, the benefit of others, and the eternal rewards of heaven?

All of this boils down to matters of the heart, and the one to whom we will give an account is Jesus, the One who sees and knows the heart. He didn't come to earth the first time to judge trivial matters or family disputes, but we will one day stand before him as Judge when he comes again. And it will be to the delight of the one whose heart is upright in these matters to hear the words "Well done, good and faithful servant."

There is nothing wrong with being wealthy or successful, but with great blessing comes great responsibility. And for those who use their blessing to bless others, there is even greater reward—both in this life and in the life to come. "For where your treasure is, there your heart will be also" (Luke 12:34).

13

"This Is My Body"

Whoever, therefore, eats the bread or drinks the
cup of the Lord in an unworthy manner will be
guilty concerning the body and blood of the Lord.

—1 Corinthians 11:27 ESV

I wonder what it would've been like to have been with
Jesus when he lived on earth. What was it like to hear the
power of God in his voice? He had an authority unlike
anyone people had ever heard before, even their own leaders.
The Scriptures tell us many were filled with awe, wonder,
and amazement.

How awesome it must have been to see Jesus raise someone from the dead. An atmosphere of grief was changed in
an instant. One minute people were weeping, the next they
were rejoicing. A mother received her son back; a father saw

his daughter open her eyes again. Sisters saw their brother emerge from a tomb four days after his death.

The disciples were firsthand witnesses to these miracles. There was so much to process, so much to take in. Surely there were times when it was overwhelming, making it difficult to piece together and comprehend. Only later, after they were given the Holy Spirit, were they able by that Spirit to remember, see things clearer, and understand.

Of the Twelve Jesus uniquely chose, he brought three even closer—Peter, James, and John. They are known as the inner circle, or the inner three. They heard and saw things no one else did, including Jesus being transfigured in eye-piercing light on a mountain as he spoke with Moses and Elijah, who visited him from heaven.[1]

The four gospel accounts give us all we need to know concerning who Jesus is, what he modeled and taught, and what he ultimately fulfilled and accomplished for us by going to the cross and being raised to life. But surely there is so much more that happened than what the gospel accounts record for us. John ended the writing of his gospel by saying, "There are also many other things that Jesus did, which, if they were written one by one, I suppose not even the world itself could contain the books that would be written" (John 21:25).

I am curious to know what those things are. But I suppose I will have to wait until the day I see him face-to-face. By then, the things of the past may not matter anymore because of the complete satisfaction of being in his presence.

This is what the Christian ultimately longs for: the presence of Christ. This is why Paul, perhaps the greatest Christian who ever lived, said "to depart and be with Christ" would be far better than any fruitful life or ministry he could have on earth (Philippians 1:22–23).

Death, for the Christian, should never be seen as punishment, but rather as a promotion. It is simply the next phase in God's redemptive plan to bring us to the glory he intends for us, the glory of being like him, worshiping him, and being in his presence.

Either we will see his face when we die or when he returns to earth, whichever comes first. But until that day comes, we can still experience him to a certain degree through the power of the indwelling Holy Spirit, who lives in all who place their faith and trust in Jesus.

There are many different ways Christians can *spiritually* experience the love and presence of Christ today, whether by prayer, worship, service, Bible reading and study, or relationships with other Christians. One unique way we can experience his spiritual presence is when the church gathers together to share in what is traditionally known as the Lord's Supper, the Eucharist, or Holy Communion. This is the service of remembrance Jesus instituted with his disciples on the night before he was crucified in Jerusalem—a service that Christians still participate in today as we remember the body and blood of Christ given in sacrifice for us on the cross.

There has been widespread confusion within some Christian circles as to what Jesus actually meant when he held up a piece of bread and said, "This is my body," and then held up a cup of wine and said, "This is my blood."

Within Roman Catholic circles, there is the belief that what Jesus said he meant literally. Each time a Catholic church celebrates the Mass, where they partake of the wafer and the wine, they believe they are partaking of the *actual body* and the *actual blood* of Christ. Somehow, mysteriously, the actual substance of the bread and wine is supernaturally changed into the literal body and blood of Christ, even though the human senses do not perceive that change in taste or appearance.

This means that every time the Catholic Church celebrates the Mass they are in fact offering up Christ as a sacrifice on a regular basis, and that somehow in a literal sense Christ is in this way manifested on earth. But is this consistent with what Scripture teaches elsewhere, and was this Jesus' intent when he held the bread and the cup before his disciples?

Understanding this is pivotal to understanding the true nature of the cross, and it is here that the book of Hebrews is perhaps the most helpful. The background of the book comes from the Old Testament practice of the sacrificial system given by Moses, whereby the priests of Israel would offer up sacrifices to temporarily atone for the sins of the people.

The seriousness of sin before a holy God demanded a just consequence, and the Bible teaches that "the wages of sin is death" (Romans 6:23). But the animals that were sacrificed were not sufficient to atone for *human* sin; only a sinless human could do that, and therefore those sacrifices were short term, a type of a better sacrifice to come.

This ongoing practice in the Old Testament was designed to foreshadow the future perfect sacrifice of Jesus Christ, whereby his body and blood offered on the cross was designed to be a *permanent* satisfactory atonement for human sin. Jesus offered himself deliberately to pay the penalty our sins deserved. His sacrifice satisfied the demands of justice because God's holiness was offended by our sin.

Therefore, dying in our place, God's wrath was satisfied for the believing sinner who embraces Jesus as his or her Savior and Lord. This sacrifice, writes the author of Hebrews, was done once by Jesus, and is now completed. It was sufficient the first time, and never needs to be repeated. The author of Hebrews suggests that Jesus can be understood to be the High Priest who offered the sacrifice, as well as the sacrifice himself.

> For this is the kind of high priest we need: holy, innocent, undefiled, separated from sinners, and exalted above the heavens. He doesn't need to offer sacrifices every day, as high priests do—first for their own sins, then for those of the people. He did this once for all when He offered Himself.[2]
>
> 7:26–27

Similarly, in Hebrews 9, we are told that he first appeared to make this full and final sacrifice *one time* with the promise of coming the second time, not to atone for sin (since that has been done already), but to bring a reward of complete salvation—not just the soul, but the body as well.

> But now He has appeared one time . . . for the removal of sin by the sacrifice of Himself. And just as it is appointed for people to die once—and after this, judgment—so also the Messiah, having been offered once to bear the sins of many, will appear a second time, not to bear sin, but to bring salvation to those who are waiting for Him.
>
> vv. 26–28

This line of biblical teaching and evidence suggests there is no ongoing need for sacrifices. Not only has the sacrificial system of the Old Testament been fulfilled and set aside, there is no need for any type of service that seeks to mysteriously perform a sacrifice all over again on a regular basis. The sacrificial system is finished. Pastor and author John MacArthur explains it well:

> All the Old Testament sacrifices did was to portray and develop almost a passionate longing for the final sacrifice, which would truly take away sin. The Old Testament had a priesthood, an altar, and sacrifices, which were only shadows, anticipatory, of the final sacrifice that would come with Christ. He came, He offered that sacrifice, and God punctuated that one sacrifice by destroying the temple, using the Romans to do it in AD 70, by destroying the altars, thus smashing the entire sacrificial system of the Old Testament, and all the records of all the genealogies, of all those in the priestly line, thus ending, permanently, the priesthood. There are no more sacrifices. There are no more altars. And there are no more priests as a special order to offer sacrifices. It all came to an end at the sacrifice of Jesus Christ.[3]

We should not hold to the belief that Jesus is once again offered up as a sacrifice every time God's people gather to celebrate the bread and the cup. This would be inconsistent with the Scriptures, the goal of Christ's mission, and the nature of the cross. Atonement doesn't need to be made every week. It was made finally and completely on that dark day two thousand years ago.[4]

So in what sense are we to take the words of Jesus when he said, "This is my body" and "this is my blood"? I would suggest, as hinted at earlier, that Jesus meant this in a *symbolic* and *spiritual* sense. Surely this is how the disciples would have understood it at the time he said it, while the bread and the cup were in his hand. A commonsense explanation of this comes from Wayne Grudem:

> Jesus spoke in symbolic ways many times when speaking of himself. He said, for example, "I am the true vine" (John 15:1), or "I am the door; if any one enters by me, he will be saved" (John 10:9), or "I am the bread which came down from heaven" (John 6:41). In a similar way, when Jesus says, "This is my body," he means it in a symbolic way, not in an actual, literal, physical way. In fact, as he was sitting with his disciples holding the bread, the bread was in his hand but it was distinct from his body and that was, of course, evident to the disciples. None of the disciples present would have thought that the loaf of bread that Jesus held in his hand was actually his physical body, for they could see his body before their eyes. They would have naturally understood Jesus' statement in a symbolic way. Similarly, when Jesus said "This cup which is poured out for you is the new covenant in my blood" (Luke 22:20), he certainly did not mean that the cup was actually the new covenant, but that the cup represented the new covenant.[5]

This is the best way to understand this biblical practice of believers regularly sharing in the bread and the cup. It is a symbolic remembrance of the sacrificial death of Christ. The apostle Paul wrote, "For as often as you eat this bread and drink the cup, you proclaim the Lord's death until He comes" (1 Corinthians 11:26).

The Lord's Supper is both a reminder and a proclamation of the good news found in the cross—that sin is atoned for and forgiveness can be found in the person and work of Jesus

Christ. But even more than that, there is spiritual fellowship with Christ and spiritual fellowship with other believers that is experienced in its partaking.

The fellowship we have with Christ and all the blessings and promises associated with it is brought to us through the power of the Holy Spirit. And all those who believe and who have the Holy Spirit can experience fellowship with Jesus and with one another as they share in this service of remembrance and proclamation.

This experience is often called a "means of grace," whereby in this context we sense the cleansing power of God to renew and refresh our fellowship with him as we confess our sins and remember what he has done for us on the cross. It reminds us that in a very real way we are spiritually united to Christ and to one another as his church.

So it is a tradition within the church to come to the Lord's Supper with a willingness to "examine" ourselves (1 Corinthians 11:27–29), repenting and confessing our sins before God so that any fellowship that has been strained from unconfessed sin can be restored by the forgiving grace of God.

These times of fellowship with Jesus can be quite powerful and moving if done with a sincere and humble heart of faith. I have personally walked away from a time of Communion with a refreshed heart as I remember how much Jesus loves me, even to the point of dying in my place. What wondrous love is this that my God should leave his home in glory and come to this fallen world to take our place in the most horrendous death ever devised by man!

To meditate on that reality can be nourishing to one's soul. Professor J. Todd Billings describes it well when he says that preaching, baptism, and the Lord's Supper are "material signs and seals of God's covenant promise, through which the Risen Christ communicates his person and benefits by the power of the Spirit."[6]

Symbolism? Yes. But much more than that, these are the means of grace that spiritually connect our souls to our Savior, who today is seated at the right hand of the throne of God, awaiting his return to earth at the appropriate time. (See Hebrews 1:3, 13; 8:1; 10:12; 12:2.) Interestingly, the fact that he is seated on the throne in heaven communicates that his sacrificial work as High Priest is done.

Christians differ on how often we should experience the Lord's Supper and the spiritual nourishment it brings. Some churches practice it every week, others once a month, still others once a quarter or as little as twice a year. I've served and worshiped in churches that have done it in all those frequencies described, and my personal preference is to share in it at least once a month.

The Bible seemingly leaves this open, without prescribing an explicit command on the frequency of the practice, though there are those who might make their own case against that idea. But most Christians do agree that the Lord's Supper is something that only Christians should engage in, since it is a sign of faith in and unity with Jesus Christ and his sacrifice for us. It is also a sign of unity with God's people, of communion and community with the church, which is metaphorically called the body of Christ.

So when we come to the table, we should come with humility, faith, contrition, an examined heart, confessing lips, a thankful and worshipful attitude, and a desire to be right with God and reconciled with our brothers, sisters, and neighbors so that we don't "eat the bread or drink the cup of the Lord in an unworthy manner" (1 Corinthians 11:27 ESV).

The Lord's Supper is both a sign of and the means of experiencing our unity with Christ and his church. And all this comes through the Spirit of Christ, the Holy Spirit.

Interestingly, we might think the disciples had a distinct advantage, since they were able to see Jesus firsthand, but Jesus said it would be better for them if he went away so that he could send the Holy Spirit, who would remain with them, and who would apply all the blessings and benefits of his saving work (John 16:7).

In this way, we are blessed in a unique way today, even though we do not yet see him face-to-face. But that day will come soon enough, my friend. So get ready, because the time is getting shorter. For those who truly believe, there will be a day when you will hear his voice, touch his hands and feet, look into his face, and embrace your King, knowing that all is well.

And the voice you hear will hopefully utter the words "Well done, good and faithful servant." The same voice that on the cross uttered the words "It is finished," because the sacrifice for sin was accomplished once and for all.

14

Blasphemy of the Holy Spirit

"He will glorify me, for he will take what is mine and declare it to you."

—John 16:14 ESV

You've likely heard the catchy commercial phrase *Buy one, get one*, also known by the acronym BOGO. Our local grocery store here in Florida regularly advertises BOGO specials, and this—along with their high-quality bakery—keeps me coming back.

However, I remember being puzzled when I first heard the phrase *Buy one, get one*. I thought, *Of course, that makes sense. When you buy one, you actually get one.*

My confusion was heightened even more one day when I was at a Toronto Blue Jays spring training baseball game. A vendor walking up and down the aisles, selling ice-cold refreshments, would call out, "Buy one, get . . . [with a long pause] . . . one." People would laugh, and I couldn't figure out why. They were waiting for another word, a word that never came.

It was then that my friend introduced me to the common understanding of the phrase: *Buy one, get one free.* Suddenly it all made sense. One little word gave me perspective on the entire phrase, and I realized the acronym BOGO was just a *shortened* way of communicating it.

As we have touched on throughout this book, certain phrases can seemingly have one meaning on the surface, but when you take a deeper look, you gain a fuller or very different understanding.

One such phrase is the biblical concept *blasphemy of the Holy Spirit.* The word *blasphemy* doesn't come up much in conversation today, mostly because our culture does not fear God like it used to. The word itself means "to speak evil of" or "to curse the name of God." The idea behind it is that it is a sin to slander God, attribute evil to him, or in a careless fashion, mock something that is sacred to him (sacrilege).

This is what the Pharisees accused Jesus of doing when he was forgiving sin, making claims to be equal to the Father, or acknowledging he was the Christ, the Son of God (Luke 5:21; John 10:30–31; Matthew 26:63–66).

Jesus was merely a man in their eyes, just another "sinner" who took liberties when it came to their sacred customs and man-made laws. For them, he could never be God because they could never conceive of the idea that God could or would ever lower himself, taking on human form, even though the Scriptures foretold this, especially the prophet Isaiah. So for them, Jesus was a blasphemer, and everything he did and claimed to do in the name of God was blasphemous.

But little did they realize that Jesus was not the one who was committing blasphemy, but the Pharisees. And not only were they blasphemous toward Jesus and the heavenly Father, Jesus also said they were blasphemous toward the third person of the Trinity, the Holy Spirit.

A story that is often misunderstood and misused is found in three of the gospel accounts: Matthew 12:22–32, Mark 3:22–27, and Luke 11:17–23, with only minor details added or omitted, depending on which gospel you are reading.[1] For our purposes, we will look at the Matthew account, since it is one of the most detailed.

Jesus had just healed a demon-possessed man who was also blind and mute. As you can imagine, for the man, it was quite a deliverance from the realm of darkness, both spiritually and physically. The crowds were dumbfounded, or "astounded," as Matthew put it, and wondered if Jesus was their long-awaited Messiah.

But the Pharisees were quick to try to stomp out that idea. They implicitly denied any heavenly miracle by rapidly attributing Jesus' actions to the devil, saying, "The man drives out demons only by Beelzebul, the ruler of the demons" (Matthew 12:24). The title *Beelzebul*, or *Beelzebub*, was a name given to an ancient heathen deity who was said to be the prince or ruler of all evil spirits, mainly the devil or Satan himself.

In essence, the Pharisees accused Jesus of being possessed by Satan and attributed his powers over the spiritual realm, nature, sickness, or diseases as nothing less than satanic or demonic in nature. Logically this made little sense, and Jesus (who knew their thoughts) countered their accusation by asserting that any kingdom or house divided against itself would collapse. "If Satan casts out Satan" (12:26 ESV), then he is fighting against himself and his kingdom will not stand.

Of course, his point is that the only logical conclusion is that his power comes not from Satan but from God, namely the Holy Spirit, who has supernaturally empowered him to do these miracles as a testimony to who he is as the Messiah who has come.

Here then comes the idea of an unpardonable or unforgivable sin. Jesus said,

> Because of this, I tell you, people will be forgiven every sin and blasphemy, but the blasphemy against the Spirit will not be forgiven. Whoever speaks a word against the Son of Man, it will be forgiven him. But whoever speaks against the Holy Spirit, it will not be forgiven him, either in this age or in the one to come.
>
> Matthew 12:31–32

The point Jesus is making is this: Any and all sins are forgivable, except one. Careless words that are spoken, acts of immorality, gossip, sinful anger (to name a few), or even words spoken against Christ himself are all forgivable, assuming that one later repents and receives Christ as Lord. *Let us be clear: There is no sin too great that God's grace cannot cover it and rescue someone from the grips of evil.* Salvation and cleansing are available to all, even a thief on a cross.

But one sin will not be forgiven, and the Pharisees were committing that very sin: One cannot deliberately reject that which is obviously from God, concerning the person and work of Jesus Christ. The Pharisees had heard him speak, they watched him do miracles, and they could not catch him

147

saying anything false or bringing harm to any person he laid hands on or healed by his spoken word.

It was obvious. Jesus was exactly who he claimed to be, and he had the words and actions to prove it. Yet in spite of all this evidence, the Pharisees still willfully and purposefully rejected him and attributed his miracles not to the power of God but to the power of Satan.

This is tantamount to a wholesale rejection of the Holy Spirit's testimony about who Jesus truly is as the Messiah, Son of God, and Savior of the world. All throughout his ministry, when Jesus preached with power, healed the sick, raised the dead, and so on, the Holy Spirit was testifying loud and clear through these things that Jesus was the Christ.

In fact, Jesus later said this is the Holy Spirit's purpose: to bring glory to Christ (John 16:14). His job is to shine the light on Jesus. And this is what he was doing. These Pharisees saw this with their own eyes, yet they still rejected Christ and blasphemed the testimony of the Holy Spirit concerning Jesus.

But one may ask, How can this be an unforgivable sin *today*, when Jesus is not here on earth doing and saying these things now like he was then?

To be technical about it, this kind of blasphemy is not happening in the *exact* same way it was happening then, because Jesus is no longer on earth in the flesh doing miracles, but is now in heaven sitting at the right hand of the Father. Therefore, one cannot reject him from a firsthand eyewitness stance like the Pharisees did.

But *it is still* happening in one sense today, when a person rejects the Holy Spirit's testimony about Jesus that comes through God's people and the Word of God by means of the message of the gospel. Today the Holy Spirit still testifies to who Jesus is through the written Word of God (Scripture) and through the spoken message of Christ's life, death, and resurrection that makes up the content of the gospel of God's grace.[2] Without this gospel, people will remain lost in their unbelief, which is ultimately a rejection of Christ.

And if a person dies in unbelief, there is no forgiveness for sin.

This is what it means to blaspheme the Holy Spirit. Unfortunately, this is not always the way blasphemy of the Holy Spirit is understood. Some erroneously think it is a rejection of the Holy Spirit's existence altogether, which is indeed a form of blasphemy, but not the kind of blasphemy we are talking about in this context.

Still others may think that blasphemy of the Holy Spirit is a refusal to believe in miracles today, which is very problematic, but is still not the kind of unforgivable blasphemy that Jesus is talking about in our passage under consideration.

To be fair, there are some "counterfeit miracles" today that happen in many churches that we should have a right to be suspect of, especially if they are done by someone who is a known false teacher or are not in keeping with biblical precedent or a proper understanding of the signs and wonders that were unique to the ministry of the apostles (see 2 Corinthians 12:12).

Personally, I believe that every time someone repents of their sin and trusts in Christ alone for their salvation we see an incredible miracle of a spiritually dead heart being born again and made alive toward God. Not to mention the common grace that God gives through modern medicine to heal in ways never seen before in human history.

Getting things wrong about the Holy Spirit is forgivable, but rejecting his testimony about Jesus (which results in an ongoing rejection of Jesus himself) is not one of them. My prayer is that God's people will be bold in these last days so that more unbelief is overcome and this sin will become less common.

If there is one thing all of this teaches us, it is that we need to go deeper in context in order to understand biblical words and phrases correctly so they can be applied appropriately. Not everything on the surface is what it seems. My big concern is that the church today suffers from a lot of surface-level teaching that is mostly thematic in nature. And when the theme becomes primary, then many Bible verses are picked from various places without much attention to their context.

This has the potential to be dangerous. Why? Because some speakers may pull select Scripture verses out of context to promote their own personal agenda, disregarding faithfulness to their context. This does not mean, however, that your pastor should never do a thematic study from the pulpit. Sometimes such a series is necessary to address specific issues that are relevant and to look at those issues from a whole-Bible perspective.

But one advantage of expository preaching in a verse-by-verse fashion is that a pastor over time models for his congregation how to interpret Scripture in context, so that popular themes, terms, and ideas that are commonplace in the church can be understood correctly and applied faithfully through the sound interpretive principles that are modeled.

No matter what approach your pastor takes in the pulpit, context matters. No matter what kind of Bible study you are a part of, context matters. When the book of the law was found after the exile of Israel, the people were starving for the Word of God to be preached again. And the Levites were tasked with explaining God's commands from the time when they were given to Moses. "They read from the book, from the Law of God, clearly, and they gave the sense, so that the people understood the reading" (Nehemiah 8:8 ESV).

In other words, the Levites translated and taught the Word in context, giving background and meaning, so that the people could understand the words of God correctly. This should be the church's task today so that we have a deeper and truer understanding of terms and phrases that often only get a surface interpretation.

Shallow teaching will breed shallow Christians, and what you win them with is what you win them to. Therefore, we have an obligation to go deeper so that we can foster a culture where Christians are discerning and trained in the ways and words of God.

CONCLUSION

Handle With Care—Using Scripture Appropriately

The Word of God is precious. It is a gift to us from God that gives us God's heart, God's voice, God's plan, and God's will. It is of utmost importance that we seek to embrace sound interpretive principles in order to hear its message correctly in the context of our believing, Spirit-filled community.

Understanding the cultural, historical, and grammatical issues that go into biblical interpretation can be challenging at times. But we should never abandon the literal (plain sense) meaning of Scripture, following the rules of grammar with specific attention given to the style or genre of the literature we are seeking to interpret. With the Holy Spirit at work in our hearts to illuminate the text, we can approach this task in faith that God's Word is still speaking to us. Only then can we better know the author's original intent and what it meant to those who first heard or read it so that we can better apply those principles.

But it is often the case that these principles are ignored or set aside due to ignorance or modern-day tendencies to read or use the Bible for modern-day agendas.

In the course of this book, we have seen several ways Bible stories can be misread, misused, or misunderstood. We should be on our guard against the following list of errors that could steer us in the wrong direction.

- **Ignoring the context.** This is perhaps the most common mistake when it comes to misused or misinterpreted verses or stories. Taking anything out of context is almost always going to give us a false interpretation of the truths God intends for us to understand and apply to our lives. Furthermore, comprehension of the nature and genre of a book, such as the historical book of Acts or the apocalyptic symbolism in a prophetic book like Revelation, will help us more faithfully discern a text in context.

- **Misunderstanding the main point.** Many preachers, for the sake of seeking to connect emotionally or pragmatically with their audience, put the main emphasis of a Bible story in the wrong place, essentially eclipsing the main point of any given text. Zacchaeus was curious, but the story is more about Jesus seeking him rather than the other way around. True, there are interesting and applicable side notes that can be discerned from studying God's Word, but let us never miss the main point God wants us to get, lest we make the Bible into a

154

practical how-to guide instead of a book that highlights the glory and character of God and his saving plan for us. The story of Jonah is about God and his pursuing grace, not about Jonah himself or a big fish.

- **Reading modern-day biases into the text.** All of us are biased. We all come to the interpretive task with baggage and preconceived notions of reality. The trick is to know what our biases actually are, and with the best of intentions seek to put our modern-day tendencies aside in an effort to enter into the biblical worldview of the time these documents were written. This may mean that we imagine ourselves as first-century Jews with all the customs and traditions associated with that worldview so that we can better hear the Word of God in its original context. Bible study aids can truly help us hear the author's original intent and help us discover what our modern-day biases may actually be.

- **Dismissing discovered truth that goes against what we already believe or think.** Often modern-day thinking and agendas will be offended by biblical truths. Words like *submission* or subjects like homosexuality are controversial to modern-day minds. But the Bible and what it teaches can serve as a corrective to our philosophical objections, such that we should be committed to pursuing the way God thinks about our world instead of what we want our world to be. Our sinful flesh will always be offended by the gospel and its claims on us, but surrendering to God's way of thinking frees us to live the abundant life.

- **Allowing tradition to clouds the facts.** Many people make the mistake of taking a human tradition and imposing that tradition back onto their own understanding of Scripture, without checking the factuality of that tradition with the text itself. The story of the wise men is a perfect example of this.

- **Reading into parables what is not really there.** Parables were stories Jesus told that contained hidden spiritual truths about the kingdom—truths that can only be discerned through the eyes of faith and deeper study, and we should avoid reading them allegorically as if each participant in the story stood for something else hidden that is not obvious. By design, their spiritual insights were hidden from the unbelieving heart. But for those with ears to hear and eyes to see, they shed a powerful light on the principles of the kingdom that God intends the believer to know and live by.

- **Ignoring what the Bible teaches elsewhere on any given topic.** Sometimes more light is shed on a Bible story or idea when we look at what the Bible teaches about it in another section of Scripture. For example, we learned so much more about how to interpret the Cain and Abel story by looking at what the Bible teaches about it later, in Hebrews 11. Such is often the case—we must consider the whole counsel of God when it comes to interpreting and applying principles derived from these stories. The Bible sheds more light on things than what we may initially grasp. Since the Holy Spirit is the inspiration and authority behind all that is written in Scripture, we can expect him to help us by giving us a consistent message and further clarification as we study.

- **Giving new meaning to words and ideas that are not consistent with God's Word.** This is the tactic of many false teachers and cults, using Christian words without Christian definitions. Even importing a new meaning for phrases like *sowing your seed* is another way to mislead someone. Word studies themselves are helpful, but can be limited because words may mean something different in a different context. Again, context is crucial, and knowing how a biblical author is using a term or phrase is essential to correct interpretation. This is especially true for the term *baptism of the Holy Spirit*.

- **Missing the plain-sense meaning of a text or ignoring figurative language.** We should always seek to interpret the Bible literally unless it is obvious that figurative or symbolic language is being used (which some genres, such as apocalyptic literature, may include or employ more often). When Jesus said, "This is my body" as he held the bread up before the disciples at the Last Supper, it was obvious that he was speaking figuratively. The same is true for when he told the disciples that if your hand causes you to sin, "cut it off." He was obviously not speaking literally, but making a spiritual point to cut sin out of your life through true repentance.

- **Taking a man-centered approach instead of seeing God and his glory as the central focus of Scripture.** Remember that the Bible is primarily a book about God. The Bible is God's revelation of himself and his saving plan for us, which makes it more about him. We all need application to fill our lives so that we can live faithfully, but knowing the person and character of God is what will sustain us in this life and the life to come. Each time we come to a text, we should ask ourselves, "What does this teach me about God?" Only after we have discovered what that is should we look at ourselves as individuals and as a church to know how we should live.

Much more could be said about interpreting Scripture correctly. These ten ideas are not meant to be exhaustive. But my hope is that knowing these stumbling blocks and reading these stories in context will help you in your journey of discovering God, his heart, and his plan for your life.

None of us are perfect, and there are times when our understanding of God's Word may change as we grow spiritually and study more. Surely we are to grow up and cast aside ignorant understandings or false conclusions that were made in error or without full knowledge of the context. Though we may change, God's Word never does. It stands forever. You can have faith that God's promises will be fulfilled, because they are rooted in the very character of God himself, who never changes.

People are hungry for truth but don't always realize it until their soul craves it. But the ability to discern God's truth can only come as a result of the work of the Holy Spirit in the heart. My prayer is that this book will be an aid to the student of the Word who seeks to understand it better so that they may live a more faithful life.

But more than that, my desire is that you will hunger to know God the way he has revealed himself in the pages of his Word. A right view of God will transform us and renew our minds so that we are better equipped to carry out the mission of the gospel he has called the church to bring to a lost and dying world.

Let us strive to be faithful, and in humility, allow ourselves to be corrected along the way.

ACKNOWLEDGMENTS

God has a way of sovereignly weaving all things to-gether for good for those who love him and are the called ones according to his purpose (Romans 8:28). My journey of faith has led me to paths that have had un-expected twists and turns, with many joys and heartaches that have made me into the Christ-follower that I am today. Anyone who has walked with the Lord for a length of time will likely have a similar testimony. But one thing always remains constant: God is faithful, and he is good and kind, and the various experiences that accompany our faith journey may change us, but they will never change him. He is the immovable, unchangeable, unshakable God.

His goal is to make us like his Son (Romans 8:29), and my prayer is that this book will be but a small aid in that process so that we may increasingly learn to think like God thinks as we allow the Word of God to shape our minds and hearts.

In 2015, I stepped away from pastoral ministry in order to teach full-time and write while also spending more time with my beloved wife, Jennifer, and the two boys who bring joy to our home, my sons Joshua and Andrew. Though there are days when the urge to preach still courses through my veins, my life calling to teach and shepherd God's people now finds its fulfillment in the classrooms of the college and the local church, as well through my pen and keyboard.

There are several people in the last few years who have had a dynamic influence in my life and have encouraged me in my ministry. I truly believe my wife, Jennifer, has been one of the greatest gifts a God-fearing man could ask for. Her prayers, her joy in Jesus, and her love for people, along with her servant heart bring God's grace and blessing into our home. Each day with her reminds me how good God is.

There are many whose continual prayers and wise counsel have aided me spiritually as well as in the tasks of teaching and writing, but especially Don and Donna Hart, two of the best biblical counselors I have ever met. I am also reminded of the faithful encouragement of those who attend my Thursday evening Bible studies at Calvary Church Eastlake in Tarpon Springs, Florida. Our study times are rich and have often closed with all of us gripped by the greatness of God.

I find great joy in the support and camaraderie of my fellow faculty and staff at Trinity College of Florida, where I teach Bible and Theology and lead the Honors Program. Dr. Thomas Woodward has been a constant encourager in pursuing great things for God as together we have shared many teaching ministry opportunities that make teaching a joy.

At Calvary Church in Clearwater, where I worship and serve under the excellent pastoral leadership of Dr. Willy Rice, I have found a group of Christians who are hungry for the Word. They are eager to serve and to see the kingdom of God grow. May the Lord be glorified in his church through the faithful preaching of his Word and by those who give their lives to build up the body of Christ.

NOTES

Chapter 2: Gideon and His Fleece

1. Judges 2:15. Sometimes God uses rather unexpected means to get our attention.

2. This is what is called a *theophany*, which is a temporary manifestation of God himself on the earth. To be even more specific, this occurrence of the Angel of the Lord is likely a *Christophany*, which is a preincarnate appearance of Jesus Christ, the second person of the Trinity.

3. These insights into Gideon's heart and his inner struggles prior to his acceptance of and fulfilling God's call come from a sermon by Dr. William Rice, "The Things That Could Be," January 3, 2016, Calvary Church, Clearwater, Florida.

4. The idea that if man saw God face-to-face he would die is from Exodus 33:20, where Moses met with God on Mount Sinai but was unable to see God in his fullness or absolute holiness. As fallen sinners, we must be made perfect before we encounter God in this way, which makes us long for heaven.

5. John MacArthur, *Found: God's Will* (Colorado Springs: David C. Cook, 1977), 58.

Chapter 3: Cain and Abel

1. Kenneth Mathews, *The New American Commentary, Genesis 1–11:26* (Nashville: Broadman & Holman, 1996), 257.

2. Victor Hamilton notes the text highlights Abel's "firstfruits" offering whereas there is no mention of Cain's offering being of the "firstfruits." However, "the text does not indict Cain for not presenting the firstfruits." Victor Hamilton, *The Book of Genesis, Chapters 1-17: The New International Commentary on the Old Testament* (Grand Rapids, MI: William B. Eerdmans, 1990), 223.

3. Mathews, *New American Commentary, Genesis 1–11:26*, 268.

4. Hamilton, *The Book of Genesis, Chapters 1–17*, 232.

5. Mathews, *Genesis 1–11:26*, 278.

Chapter 4: Jonah and the Big Fish

1. The Bible never says Jonah was swallowed by a whale, though it may be the most likely candidate based on our current maritime knowledge.

2. I wonder if there is an area of your life that God has been convicting your spirit about, but you might not be listening, or worse yet, you're not willing to listen. But God won't go away. Jonah knew what was right, and he didn't do it. My hope is that we will listen to God when conviction comes, so we don't end up at the bottom like Jonah.

3. Wayne Grudem provides this helpful definition of repentance in his *Systematic Theology: An Introduction to Biblical Doctrine* (Grand Rapids. MI: Zondervan, 1994), 713.

Chapter 5: The Woman Caught in Adultery

1. Interestingly, this supposed excuse for sin—"I'm only human"—is a misnomer. For Jesus was fully human, yet without sin (Hebrews 4:15). Further, prior to the fall, both Adam and Eve were without sin and were rightly considered to be fully human. Therefore, the phrase "I'm only human" is merely an excuse for a sinful life in a fallen world. For in the new heaven and the new earth, when we are made morally perfect and have received our glorified, resurrected bodies, we will be fully human in the ideal sense.

2. There is more than one controversy surrounding this story. Many question whether it was part of the original Scriptures or if it was added later by a scribe and not John himself. It is not found in many early manuscripts. Furthermore, the words and vocabulary used don't sound like John, even though that is not an automatic disqualifier. Many of the

early church fathers in the centuries after the early church do not quote or comment on this passage either. Still, even after all of this, the weight of evidence suggests that the story is authentic because it fits the literary flow of the book of John and seems to characterize Jesus in a consistent manner with the rest of the book. According to his commentary, William Hendriksen states that a disciple of John named Papias may have authenticated this story. For within the pages of the ancient historian Eusebius's book *Ecclesiastical History*, he states, "The same writer (Papias) has expounded another story about a woman who was accused before the Lord of many sins. . . ." *Ecclesiastical History*, III, xxxix, 17, in Hendriksen, *John: New Testament Commentary* (Grand Rapids, MI: Baker Book House, 1953), 35. Hendriksen also states that St. Augustine, in the fourth century, "stated definitively that certain individuals had removed from their codices the section regarding the adulteress, because they feared women would appeal to this story as an excuse for their infidelity" (ibid.).

3. The Bible says the "wages of sin is death" and so it is God's prerogative to decide when and how to execute this sentence. The fact that he is often patient with us, wanting us to come to repentance, is itself an act of his grace. Stoning was God's chosen punishment at the time in an effort to impress upon his people the absolute holiness of his character and their need to keep themselves from the stain of sin, particularly the sins of the neighboring adulterous Canaanites. It obviously would serve as a deterrent.

Chapter 7: Zacchaeus

1. In John 6:14–15, the crowds at one point, after seeing his miracle of feeding the 5,000, were interested in making him their king by force. Truly they were looking for a miracle worker who could lead them and deliver them from their oppressors just like Moses did in leading their deliverance from ancient Egypt. The feeding of the 5,000 reminded them of the manna experience under Moses in the wilderness. Therefore, they made the connection that Jesus was the "prophet who was to come" that Moses had promised them (John 6:14). But a political and militant movement was not what Jesus came to lead. Spiritual deliverance was of more importance, and it had to be accomplished before the Lord returns a second time as triumphant King.

2. After the Israelites had defeated and burned the ancient city of Jericho, Joshua pronounced a curse on anyone who would choose to rebuild the city, saying, "Cursed before the Lord is the man who rises up and builds this city of Jericho; with the loss of his firstborn he shall lay its foundation, and with the loss of his youngest son he shall set up its gates" (Joshua 6:26 NASB). History proves that this curse came to fruition in the days of King Ahab, when a man by the name of Hiel rebuilt the city and lost his first and youngest sons when he laid the foundations and set up its gates (1 Kings 16:34).

3. John MacArthur, *The MacArthur New Testament Commentary, Luke 18–24* (Chicago: Moody Publishers, 2014), 72.

4. Ferrell Jenkins, "Zacchaeus Climbed Up into a Sycamore Tree," blog post dated October 10, 2008. Accessed May 26, 2016, https://ferrelljenkins .wordpress.com/2008/10/10/zaccheus-climbed-up-into-a-sycamore-tree/.

5. New Testament scholar Gary Burge writes, "We have no suggestion that Zacchaeus needs to repent, nor does the story imply a conversion on his part . . . as Joel Green remarks, 'On this reading, Zacchaeus does not resolve to undertake new practices, but presents for Jesus' evaluation his current behavior regarding money,'" Gary M. Burge, *Encounters With Jesus* (Grand Rapids, MI: Zondervan, 2010), 68. Further, Burge suggests that Zacchaeus "is not what everyone has assumed. He has been honest; he is collecting what is demanded without corruption and abuse" (ibid.). Unfortunately, this type of reading of the story eclipses Luke's entire point in the narrative, which is seen in the last verse (v. 10), which we will turn to shortly.

6. Elsewhere in Scripture, the scribes and Pharisees claimed Abraham as their father, but Jesus made it clear that even though they were Jews, they could not claim Abraham as their father (especially in the spiritual sense). Rather, he said, "You are of your father the Devil" (John 8:44), revealing that a true son of Abraham is a son by faith not by descent.

Chapter 8: Sowing Your Seed

1. John Piper, "Six Keys to Detecting the Prosperity Gospel," an interview dated April 14, 2014, as found at http://www.desiringgod.org/interviews/six-keys-to-detecting-the-prosperity-gospel.

2. For a helpful book on this, see Tim Challies, *The Discipline of Spiritual Discernment* (Wheaton, IL: Crossway Books, 2007).

3. See the insights of David W. Jones in his blog article "Five Errors of the Prosperity Gospel," June 5, 2015, Gospel Coalition, https://www.thegospelcoalition.org/article/5-errors-of-the-prosperity-gospel.

Chapter 9: The "Three" Wise Men

1. Studying the Bible is not only important because of its ability to inform our minds of the truth about God and us, it is also necessary as a means by which the Holy Spirit transforms our minds and hearts so that we desire to live a life that pleases him. As Richard Lintz once wrote, "[The Bible] is not merely a record of God's redemption, it is an agent of redemption." For more on studying the Bible, I recommend *How to Read the Bible for All It's Worth* by Gordon D. Fee and Douglas Stuart (Grand Rapids, MI: Zondervan, 2003).

2. The Catechism of the Catholic Church states, "All who die in God's grace and friendship, but still imperfectly purified, are indeed assured of their eternal salvation; but after death they undergo purification, so as to achieve the holiness necessary to enter the joy of heaven. The Church gives the name *purgatory* to this final purification of the elect, which is entirely different from the punishment of the damned" (CCC, 1030–1031). This teaching is also accompanied by the idea that prayer and offerings of the living can shorten the time of purification of the dead, thus making this concept a fund raiser for the church.

3. King Herod was not actually a Jew, but rather a descendant of the Edomites (an Idumean), whom the Romans placed in charge as King of Judea in 40 BC.

4. D. A. Carson, *The Expositors Bible Commentary, Matthew 1–12* (Grand Rapids, MI: Zondervan, 1995), 84.

5. The fact that these were Gentiles who came to seek after the Jewish king demonstrates that the gospel is inclusive for all peoples and that God has a heart for the nations. For in Isaiah 49:6, God says through the prophet: "It is not enough for you to be My Servant raising up the tribes of Jacob and restoring the protected ones of Israel. I will also make you a light for the nations, to be My salvation to the ends of the earth."

6. Remember, the reason for the region being overpopulated at this time was due to the fact that each family was returning to their original home for purposes of the Romans census ordered by Caesar (Luke 2:1).

Chapter 10: The Betrayal of a Disciple: Judas

1. But notice even in the list of apostles that Matthew gave, he ended the list with Judas, and said that he was the one "who also betrayed Him" (Matthew 10:4).

2. Suicide does not preclude someone from salvation, as there have been many true believers in a moment of despair or weakness who have sinned in taking their own life and yet are covered by God's ongoing grace. Taking one's life is not my point here. My point is that Judas did not display any signs of repentance and faith at any point in his involvement with Jesus, especially at the end of his life, when he could have had the opportunity as feelings of remorse surfaced.

Chapter 11: The Samaritan Pentecost

1. They also say they believe in Jesus Christ. But what do you mean when you say you *believe* in Jesus? Is it that you believe he *existed* or that you believe that he is the second person of the Trinity, God's only Son, who was God in the flesh, crucified and raised from the dead, and is the only hope of salvation for all humankind who trust in and *believe* that his sacrifice alone atones for human sin?

2. For more on this and other ideas concerning the Mormon view of the afterlife, see Walter Martin, *The Kingdom of the Cults,* rev. ed. (Minneapolis: Bethany House, 1997), 240–243.

3. For more on this verse with a fuller exposition and application, see my book *The Most Misused Verses in the Bible* (Minneapolis: Bethany House, 2012), 63–70.

4. The phrase "with the Holy Spirit *and fire*" is an additional phrase that both Matthew and Luke add on to the quotation. According to the New Testament scholar D. A. Carson, "Many see this as a double baptism—one in the Holy Spirit for the righteous and one in fire for the unrepentant (cf. the wheat and the chaff in v. 12). Fire (Mal. 4:1) destroys and consumes . . . there are good reasons, however, for taking 'fire' as a

purifying agent along with the Holy Spirit. The people John is address-
ing are being baptized by him; presumably they have repented. More
important, the preposition *en* ('with') is not repeated before fire: The one
preposition governs both 'Holy Spirit' and 'fire,' and this normally suggests a unified concept, Spirit-fire or the like. Fire often has a purifying,
not destructive, connotation in the Old Testament (e.g. Isa. 1:25; Zech.
13:9; Mal. 3:2–3)." D. A. Carson, *The Expositor's Bible Commentary,
Matthew 1–12* (Grand Rapids, MI: Zondervan, 1995), 105.

    5. Someone may ask, "Why are all these quotations phrased a little differ-
ently if they are the same quotation from that moment in John's ministry?"
The answer is that all three gospel writers, Matthew, Mark, and Luke (it
seems that the John quotation could be from a different occurrence) can
be harmonized together in such a way that we understand that one author
may have included some words that Jesus said while another decided to
leave a few words or phrases out of his quotation. But pieced together,
they all represent the basic idea of what John said concerning this baptism.

    6. See Grudem, *Systematic Theology,* 766. Grudem's treatment of
the idea of the baptism of the Holy Spirit in chap. 39 of his work is to
be commended.

    7. Ibid., 768. The larger quotation by Grudem, in context, gives us
even more detail as to what is happening besides our initial baptism into
the Spirit and incorporation into the church. He writes, "'Baptism in
the Holy Spirit,' therefore, must refer to the activity of the Holy Spirit
at the beginning of the Christian life, when he gives us new spiritual life
(in regeneration) and cleanses us and gives a clear break with the power
of sin (the initial stage of sanctification). In this way, "baptism in the
Holy Spirit" refers to all that the Holy Spirit does at the beginning of
our Christian lives" (Ibid.).

    8. Grudem, *Systematic Theology,* 772.

Chapter 12: The Rich Fool

    1. Though Job lost much of his wealth, it was later restored once he
stood the test.

    2. Darrell Bock, *Luke 9:51–24:53, Baker Exegetical Commentary on
the New Testament* (Grand Rapids, MI: Baker Book House, 1996), 1149.

3. The Greek word Jesus uses for "life" is unique in that it is referring to a certain kind of life, one that is purposeful and meaningful, and not merely one of existence.

4. John MacArthur Jr., *The MacArthur New Testament Commentary, Luke 11–17* (Chicago: Moody Publishers, 2013), 134.

Chapter 13: "This Is My Body"

1. We are told that Jesus was discussing his impending death with these two men. See Luke 9:29–32. Interestingly, from this account we can surmise that both Moses and Elijah took on some kind of bodily form and were recognizable to the disciples, who had never met these men on earth. This may potentially tell us some things about the afterlife that might be interesting—that we will know people we meet in heaven even though we never met them on earth, and that while we are in heaven we are not like "ghosts" or disembodied spirits, but actually take on some kind of bodily form, though it would not be the promised resurrection body that would come later at the return of Christ.

2. Notice the contrast the author is making between an ongoing sacrifice versus a one-time sacrifice that ended sacrifices for good.

3. John MacArthur Jr., "Explaining the Heresy of the Catholic Mass, Part 1" (April 30, 2006), accessed July 21, 2016, https://www.gty.org/resources/sermons/90-318/explaining-the-heresy-of-the-catholic-mass-part-1.

4. A modification of the Catholic position was held by Martin Luther, who said that instead of the bread and wine actually *becoming* the body and blood of the Lord, Christ is present "in, with, and under" the bread taken at Communion. Wayne Grudem explains, saying, "The example sometimes given is to say that Christ's body is present in the bread as water is present in a sponge—the water is not the sponge, but is present 'in, with, and under' a sponge, and is present wherever the sponge is present . . . in response to the Lutheran view, it can be said that it too fails to realize that Jesus is speaking of a spiritual reality using physical objects to teach us when he says, 'This is my body.'" Grudem, *Systematic Theology*, 994.

5. Ibid., 992–993.

6. Todd Billings, "Sacraments," in *Christian Dogmatics: Reformed Theology for the Church Catholic*, Michael Allen and Scott R. Swain, eds. (Grand Rapids, MI: Baker Academic, 2016), 352.

Chapter 14: Blasphemy of the Holy Spirit

1. This does not mean that there are contradictory accounts, but that each gospel writer may have chosen to add to or omit some information about the account in the course of their storytelling. This is one of the advantages of having three gospel accounts of this story, because when they are all pieced together, you get a bigger picture of the event, much like you would if you interviewed several witnesses to an accident, who saw with their own eyes what took place, even if from different angles. In addition, a gospel writer may give a summary account of the event and not go into as much detail as other gospel writers.

2. Yes, it is true that we also give testimony of the gospel to unbelievers through faithful lives and good deeds that bear fruit in keeping with our repentance and faith, but a life well lived is not enough. "Faith comes from hearing, and hearing through the word of [or through the message about] Christ" (Romans 10:17 ESV). We must testify with our lips of this good news so that people can hear and believe. In addition, the creation itself is said to testify to the glory of God (Psalm 19), but that alone is insufficient to bring someone to saving faith. The gospel must be preached and believed.

Eric J. Bargerhuff, PhD, teaches in the Bible and Theology department and directs the Honors Program at Trinity College of Florida. He served in pastoral ministry for more than twenty years in churches in Ohio, Illinois, and Florida. He received his doctorate in biblical and systematic theology from Trinity Evangelical Divinity School. Eric's passion is to write systematic and practical theology for the purposes of spiritual growth and reform in the church. He is a member of the Center for Pastor Theologians (CPT) and the Evangelical Theological Society (ETS).

Eric is the author of *The Most Misused Verses in the Bible*. He also wrote *Love that Rescues: God's Fatherly Love in the Practice of Church Discipline*, which explores the grace and fatherly love of God that should be embodied in a church's efforts to restore a brother or sister in Christ who has gone astray.

Eric and his family live in Trinity, Florida.

More From
Eric J. Bargerhuff

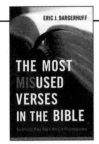

A surprising number of well-known Scripture passages are commonly misused or misunderstood. Even well-intentioned Christians take important verses out of context. In this concise yet thorough book, Pastor Eric J. Bargerhuff provides clarity in what these verses meant when they were written so we can apply them accurately today.

The Most Misused Verses in the Bible